*southern
gardens,
southern
gardening*

"... here in the arboretum below my apartment."

southern gardens, southern gardening

William Lanier Hunt

duke university press
durham, n.c.   1982

© 1982 William Lanier Hunt
First printing in paperback, 1991
Printed in the United States of America
on acid-free paper ∞
Library of Congress Cataloging-in-Publication Data
Hunt, William Lanier.
Southern Gardens, southern gardening.
Bibliography: p.
Includes index.
1. Gardening—Southern States. 1. Title.
SB453.2.S66H86 / 635.9'0975 / 81-69425
ISBN 0-8223-0463-5 AACR2
ISBN 0-8223-1233-9 (pbk.)

To Joanne Ferguson, who first conceived of
this book, edited it, and saw it through the
throes of publication.

contents

april

may

june

july

august

september

october

november

december

introduction

When my sister was a student at the University of North Carolina, she said to my mother, "There is a boy here that you would like; he brought his garden with him when he came to Chapel Hill." And that is how we came to know William Lanier Hunt, F.R.H.S., gardener and garden consultant, horticulturist and botanist; lecturer, writer, bibliophile; promoter and instigator of foundations, botanic gardens, and arboretums, and all good works in horticultural circles, here and abroad.

When Bill went to Chapel Hill in 1926 he was already a seasoned gardener. He was born (he says) and grew up in the celebrated Lindley Nursery in Greensboro, North Carolina. The nursery fields were his garden, and the greenhouses his playroom. He began to assemble his plants when he was a small boy and continued to add to his collections when he want to the Woodberry Forest School in Virginia. When he was ready to go to the university, two trucks were needed to transport his plants and rare bulbs to Chapel Hill. He rented a lot for his large iris collection, and he farmed out his bulbs and other plants in private gardens in the village. It was in these gardens that I first saw the oxblood lily, the roof iris (*Iris tectorum*), and *I. japonica*, formerly called *I. fimbriata*, a fitting name, as its petals are finely fringed; it was under that name when Bill gave it to me. He called the oxblood lily *Amaryllis advena*, but Dr. Hamilton Traub calls it *Hippeastrum bifidum*. It was once called *Rhodophiala*, and Dr. Traub has named a hybrid of the oxblood lily and another species of the same genus *Rhodophiala* ×*huntiana* and described it in the *Amaryllis Year Book* (1964) as "floribus intense rubris usque ad rhodamino-rubellis. Holotypus: Traub no. 817 a+b (TRA)."

In those days, when spring came to Chapel Hill, everyone: students, professors, botanists, horticulturists, gardeners and nature lovers, and most of the village used to walk to Laurel Hill to see the rhododendron in bloom on the slope above Morgan Creek. They called the flowers laurel, but they were really the rosebay, *Rhododendron catawbiense* var. *insularis*, though *Kalmia latifolia*, commonly called mountain laurel, also grows nearby. Here in the piedmont the flora of the mountains meets the flora of the coastal plain, and in addition to the plants growing here already, Dr. Ritchie Bell, the director of the North Carolina Botanical Garden, is establishing the major plant communities of the Carolinas so the flora from the coast to the boreal forest can be studied and enjoyed in one place; otherwise, as he says, it could be seen only by traveling two hundred miles.

One spring Bill joined the walkers to Laurel Hill; when he saw Morgan creek in its wooded slate valley with the remarkable native plants growing under the trees, he realized that the property must be preserved for the university and the state and that no time must be lost in doing it. He made up his mind to devote himself to this seemingly hopeless undertaking, although it would mean endless difficulties, disappointments and sore distress. It took twenty years and a world war (he said) to accomplish what he had set out to do, but the property was bought and paid for at last. In the meantime he had grown dozens of specimens of *Magnolia grandiflora* from seeds of superior clones found on the university campus, and had brought in and established more species of native plants, and introduced exotics from countries where the climate and growing conditions are similar to ours.

Then in 1960 he began to transfer the land to the university, as the Hunt Arboretum, to be administered under the new North Carolina Botanical Garden. When the gift was announced in 1961, Burke Davis wrote in his "Tar Heel Notebook" (*Greensboro Daily News*, November 26), that it was "one of the greatest gifts to the public weal, to be remembered as long as we are spared the thermonuclear torch. A handsome gesture indeed."

Laurel Hill as an arboretum seemed merely a dream when I first saw it. Robert Moncure, one of our rock-garden correspondents, who lived in Alexandria, Virginia, wrote that he would like to come to Raleigh on the Seaboard pullman one Saturday night, to spend Sunday with us, and return Sunday night. My Mother and I drove him to Chapel Hill Sunday afternoon. Bill took us to the Botanical Garden, and on through the briers and underbrush to Morgan Creek, where we stood on the highest hilltop, looking down on the clear, brown waters that sang as they swirled around Thomas Wolfe's rock, a ledge of purple slate two hundred feet below. The air was so still the only sound to be heard was the sound of the water, until the four o'clock chimes rang out from the Bell Tower. "Think of it," Bill said. "One hundred acres of woods and fields on the edge of the campus, and in hearing of the Bell Tower, and it's older than Kew."

In those days there was much going back and forth between gardens in Raleigh and gardens in Chapel Hill. When our garden correspondents came to visit, Bill and I passed them on. Violet Walker was our first and favorite. Bill had spent much of his school days in her garden at Woodberry, Virginia. "We called her Violent," he said,—meaning that she was as passionate as he was about plants and gardens. I call to mind these early days because Bill's writings go back to that time, when first Violet Walker and then Elizabeth Rawlinson, was the editor of *Garden Gossip* (the organ of the Garden Club of Virginia); and we all wrote for it and for each other.

Sometimes visitors came from the West: one day Lester Rowntree turned up at our door, having driven across the country in her collecting car which had only one seat—the driver's. In it she drove thousands of miles every year. She drove over hills and deserts, through forests and along the seashore, from one end of the Pacific Coast to the other. Bill and I had never seen Lester before, but we had been in correspondence with her since we read in the *Atlantic Monthly* about her camping trips in the desert, and when she arrived in North Carolina, we were already friends for life. I said, "You must go to Chapel Hill to see Bill Hunt." Lester said, "Please let me sit down a minute first." My mother said, "We are expecting you to spend the night." The next morning we went to Chapel Hill.

When we got there, Bill said to Lester, "You must go to Biltmore to see Latta Clement at the Nik-Nar nursery." Lester gave me a despairing glance. We went to the Botanical Garden and Laurel Hill and had lunch at the Inn. Then Bill gave Lester directions and a well-marked road map, and sent her on to Biltmore.

Soon after that, Bill brought Camilla Bradley to have dinner with us in Raleigh. Camilla was the editor (and moving spirit) of that remarkable and short-lived magazine, *Home Gardening for the South*, for which we both wrote, along with Caroline Dormon and her sister-in-law Mrs. James Dormon and Inez Conger and their friends in Shreveport and Jo Evans from her garden at Hapahazard Plantation. And we all wrote to each other, all of the Confederacy united as in The War. Contributors and subscribers were practically the same.

When my mother and I came to Charlotte to live, I thought we would see less of Bill, but as it turned out we saw him more often. He came, bringing with him young botanists, students or faculty of the university; he came, bringing bulbs and plants for my new garden, and once he brought a rectangular block of slate from Morgan Creek Valley. We set it, like a jewel, in a low stone wall. The valley slate is dark gray when dry, but when it rains it reveals tones of Mulberry, Mauve, and Perilla Purple.

Between visits there were letters: "We certainly do have lots of things to work on, don't we?" Bill wrote in July, 1976. "In the meantime, what source do you now know for *Iris unguicularis*? You will not believe how beautiful the new walks are, here in the arboretum below my apartment. We have made them right out into space, and dug luscious beds up and down the slopes, and planted about an acre of cyclamens. There are gorgeous trees and shrubs as well as herbaceous plants on these steep slopes where no one but a few botanists have been—ever, because they are so very steep. From the paths you can look out into treetops, and look down on the huge trunks of forest trees." I can vouch for the steepness of those slopes, for I have been dragged up and down them many times. I have seen all those cyclamens too, and the glowing yellow host of *Sternbergia lutea*.

In December there were Christmas cards reporting winter bloom: "Winter sternbergias, witch hazel, and three flowers of *Cyclamen pseudibericum*. Each year just one corm out of thirty does this." And another year, on December the 26th, "There were dozens of *Sternbergia fischeriana* the moment you left." (I think *C. pseudibericum* is tender. It never bloomed for me, but then I had only one bulb.)

While Bill was acquiring the land for his arboretum, and laying out trails, and bringing in new plants, he was also spending summers in England attending the meetings of the Royal Horticultural Society, visiting Graham Thomas's roses, and the gardens of other distinguished Fellows of the society, and haunting the London bookshops in search of rare herbals and other old English garden books, weighty volumes, mostly of folio or elephant size, some illustrated with woodcuts, and some with plates engraved and colored by hand. "Thank Heaven," Bill wrote recently, "I had the sense to sacrifice and buy Dean Herbert's *Amaryllidaceae* years ago."

Bill is not one to rest on his laurels: "At long last," he wrote in 1981, "we are going to start the Southern Garden History Society. Some months back, I re-worked the bylaws of the English society to suit fifteen Southern states. Flora Ann Bynum, John Flowers and I held several meetings winter before last, and we got the organization planned. Now, I think the first meeting could be at the Garden Symposium at Old Salem next May. Last fall I went to Natchez with Jo and Cleo to start planting the things that go with those period houses. Guess you know about the new Society at 'Calline's place.' They got it going this spring, and we are going to establish a garden of old roses there. I think I will be in Natchez this fall, and I look forward to visiting Briarwood, New Orleans, Jo Evans at Haphazard, and maybe Cleo Barnewell in Shreveport." They will be in the book.

Elizabeth Lawrence
Charlotte, North Carolina

*southern
gardens,
southern
gardening*

january

the southern winter

January is a wonderful month in the South. Snow on the magnolias one day—sunshine and winter jasmine the next. Youths skiing in the mountains—winter irises blooming in front of Rose Monroe's house in New Orleans. The first week of January is usually the coldest in the year. Even in the mid-South the thermometer may dip down to below zero, but the morning sun often brings it back up above freezing. During this first week of January, Jo Evans writes that the old-fashioned hyacinths are about to bloom in her yard at Haphazard Plantation near Natchez. Hyacinths love January down South as much as they like March in the Dutch gardens at Keukenhof. Enjoy the short southern winter while we have it; soon comes the spring and hot weather again!

The winter and spring cyclamens on my hillside have been hiding tiny buds on near-invisible stems for several weeks now. How these little stems can push up through thick oak leaves is a miracle, but they do and dare the frosts and snow. At home in the mountains around the Mediterranean, they are accustomed to the same kind of January weather we have, so the wild species from these areas adapt themselves very well to our climate in the Upper South. South of Macon, Montgomery, Jackson, Shreveport, and Dallas they need a north-facing position away from the hot sun. I am sending some to be tried even in New Orleans and Houston—but in pots where they will be high and dry! (Jo Evans thinks the muskrats ate the *Cyclamen hederifolium* she had growing up high on a cypress stump.)

Fraser's photinia is in fruit at this time of year on specimens that have enough age. A huge mass of rosy pink three hundred feet away attracted my attention last week on the campus of the University of North Carolina at Chapel Hill. It was a Fraser's photinia that had been allowed to grow without pruning, and it was a glorious sight to behold. The berries are a little pinker than those of *Photinia serrulata*, one of its parents, and almost hide the foliage. This new photinia is going to be a great addition to the berried beauties of our winters. What a wonderful feat of Dame Nature to cross the gorgeous *serrulata* with the popular "red top" (*P. glabra*) in the old nursery of the Frasers in Alabama. The new creature is even more elegant than either parent. Old nurseries have given us many such gems.

This far south, we can grow only a few firs and spruces. They give us our Christmas trees and lend a touch of the North to southern landscapes. Native pines and "cedars" (*Juniperus virginiana*) and hemlocks cheer up southern forests in winter. Arborvitaes, creeping junipers, cedars of Lebanon, and many small conifers combine with the broadleaf evergreens to enrich landscapes below Mason and Dixon's line. If your landscape loses its conifers, you will have a dull place indeed. Now is the time to plant them and brighten things up. If there is room, a group of any of the native pines will grow quickly from seedlings into bushy young trees, if they are planted in the open. Watching them grow up is a delightful experience. In full sun, they are likely to develop into large, spreading bush shapes and will remain that way up to twenty years before losing their lower branches.

Podocarpuses are such handsome evergreens that one wonders why they have not been more widely planted in the Middle and Upper South. Here, they take the place of the true yews (*Taxus*) which do not always take kindly to our heat and drought. Except in very cool shade we cannot grow English yew, that wood that supplied Edward III with the bows and arrows to defeat the French at Crécy. But podocarpuses and the upright plum yew (*Cephalotaxus*) resemble them enough to lend an Anglo-Saxon touch to the landscape.

winter tips

Open days in January are good times to prune the tangles of shrubs which have grown too thick with old and dead wood. Don't give spireas a haircut. Go over them and remove all of the dead canes and the dead parts of otherwise healthy canes. Every little piece of live wood will bloom when spring comes. The shrubs can be cut back drastically just after they flower, but everything alive that is cut off now is full of flower buds. Gardeners either let spireas get to their full size and development by pruning out only the dead wood, or they cut the bushes back right to the ground, or near it, every year in order to have somewhat smaller specimens with heavily flowered branches. In especially small places, spireas of all kinds can be maintained like this and kept good looking and healthy. If you need large cascades of white bloom, however, plant *Spiraea vanhouttei*, feed it well, and let it get as large as it will. Everybody knows this old, spreading bridal wreath that makes large fountains of white arching sprays better than any other one. It blooms with the old-fashioned white iris, blue flags, and Darwin tulips. For a change, get some pink 'Clara Butt' tulips and some other kinds that are not red and plant them next fall in this color scheme. The old red Darwin 'Farnecombe Sanders' has become too common with these other plants. 'City of Haarlem' is a beautiful, intense tulip that goes well with spireas and irises and is a bit different from the shade of red usually seen with them. 'Duc van Thol' tulips in shades of yellow are also good with this combination.

There is hardly a more useful group of spring-flowering shrubs than the spireas. After the early, delicate-flowered *S. thunbergii* blooms, and overlapping with it, comes the upright and fairly tall bridal wreath *S. prunifolia*, with its tiny double "roses." It is a mistake to try to make this tallish shrub into a rounded, short one. It will steadily send up more and more long wands that have to be cut off. It is best used at the back of shrubbery plantings or in some place where there is a narrow area in need of an early flowering, upright shrub.

S. thunbergii is a never-failing source of delight when it blooms with its wisps of tiny blossoms at daffodil time. The red or pink flowering quinces bloom at the same time and make a fine color combination during that cold, early time in the spring garden. The newer flowering quinces are now easier to get at our southern nurseries than they used to be. Everyone should investigate them because the quinces are tough shrubs that provide us with a long season of bloom. Some of the new ones come in salmon shades, and there are many different reds and pinks. There is a white form, too, that is just about the most beautiful of the more common shrubs with white flowers.

It is ridiculous to prune the quinces now, for they are just before bursting into bloom. In warm winters, they may start in January. Wait till they finish blooming. Their leaves will be out, but pruning them will not be harmful. Quinces can be shaped into a hedge, into large masses of flowering shrubs, or into more or less flat shrubs where they are up against buildings. There is nothing more glorious, however, than great tall masses of quince in the corners and backgrounds of gardens. The birds like to nest in them because the twigs are so thick that they provide a good hiding place from hawks and cats. If your quinces get scale, spray them with a dormant spray of either a miscible oil or lime sulphur. This spray should go on soon.

Of course, you will not prune your forsythias now because you can see the buds getting ready to open. Cut sprays are easy to force in water in the house. Underneath the tangled edges of the spreading varieties, the tips take root and make little new plants. These can be taken up and moved right now, and they will grow into large shrubs right away. With a small amount of work they can be espaliered against a wall. The branches do not tug at their supports like those of pyracanthas and other heavy shrubs. The only disadvantage is that the new growth has to be tied up and pruned back as the summer comes on because they keep on with lusty growth right into July!

The early daffodils are already up and in bud. To hurry a few along, put a box over them with a pane of glass in place of the bottom and keep them well watered. Daffodils of all kinds will actually develop into larger flowers after they are cut and put into water in the house than they will if they are left growing in the garden. That is one reason why they look so large in the shows. As soon as the little paper covering on each bud is split and the flower just ready to open, the buds can be cut and put in a cool room in indirect light. Here they will keep and can be held back and a few at a time brought into warmth and light to flower.

color schemes

This is the time of the year to sit down and plan color schemes for garden and grounds. If you dislike orange red quinces blooming with magenta redbuds, it is usually easier to move the quinces than the redbuds. In some gardens, there are enough flowering cherries of different shades of pink to tone down these two. White will help, too.

Gardens that are a hodgepodge of color that cannot be changed all at once can be gradually transformed by the removal of the worst offenders and the addition of plants of another color. Since there are endless beautiful color schemes that one can establish with the plants already in the landscape, it will pay to make a really serious study of what is there. Often the removal of a single bush will leave a pleasing picture. Just as often, there are several good combinations that can be achieved by the addition of new plants.

Flowering bulbs can often add exactly the color needed with a group of shrubs or perennials. A few hyacinths, here and there, are easily inserted, or a low mat of hyacinths can be planted at the foot of taller plants to make a rug of color. The daffodil 'Thalia' (*Narcissus triandrus*) flowers with redbuds just before the dogwoods take over. White masses of this tough, two-flowered daffodil can pull together a garden of many disparate colors in redbud time.

The purple-leaf plums that are so popular in the South never seem to have a real place in the scheme. Light pink is one of the colors that sets off this red violet foliage that by itself lacks vibrancy. White makes it positively colorful. Since the plum foliage is in its brightest stages all through the spring, a series of flowers from early spireas to roses can be planted where they will be seen with the plums.

The English like to put together combinations in their summer perennial gardens with the improved smoke bush (*Cotinus*). There are several violet cultivars of this foliage plant both in England and in this country. At the Cambridge Botanical Garden, which I visited last July, it was very effective planted behind perennials. Grey- and silvery-leaved plants like the artemisias are good with it, and pink is delightful with its purple foliage. In other places it was planted right in the perennial beds. One garden had pink roses in bloom with it, and the bed was faced down with the gray edger santolina spilling over a wall.

Once you get the color-scheme fever, you will go around looking at gardens everywhere with a new awareness of color. Good color schemes are restful. Mixtures are usually ineffective or boring. Discover your own color schemes, beginning with what you already have that is now ineffective and can be moved to combine well with something else.

persian-garden rugs

Those beautiful "garden rugs" you see in oriental-rug stores are not covered with fanciful designs as you might think; the gardens on them are stylized representations of real gardens.

Hidden behind the mud walls of the houses in modern Iran are beautiful little gardens crowded with the many kinds of trees and shrubs and flowers we see on their rugs. We shouldn't be surprised to find this flora so familiar to us because daffodils, pinks, tulips, irises, grapes, peaches, plums, quinces, cypresses, willows, poplars, and many other flowers, trees, and shrubs that we grow are either wild or cultivated in Iran.

Most of Iran is a hot, dry plain. Houses and gardens are protected from the heat and drying winds by high mud walls. Water is scarcer than oil! Traveling through the heat, the Persian has always dreamt of the shade and coolness of his garden—so much so that his very word for a habitation, *bagh*, means garden. The setting of much of the beautiful poetry of Persia has been a garden:

> If there is a paradise on the face of the earth,
> It is this, it is this, it is this.

Each Persian-garden rug is a pictorial map of a garden. There is usually a long channel of water (shown with stylized waves) down the middle of the rug with another channel across it, making a big cross. Paths run beside the water with small flowers growing in them. In the rectangles formed by the channels are big beds or areas of flowers—each one sometimes divided into smaller gardens—in which peacocks strut and nightingales sing. The nightingale is an Eastern symbol of love.

The trees in these gardens are cypresses (symbol of the future or of everlasting life, like our Christmas tree), willows, poplars, ashes, junipers, beeches, elms, maples, oaks, and walnuts. Vines are often shown climbing the trees and running around the edge of the rug.

For centuries, Persia had traffic with both China and Egypt. Chinese and Egyptian lotuses and Chinese willows and peaches came to be cultivated in Persia—the peach tree so intensively that European botanists, believing it to be Persian, named this Chinese native *Prunus persica*.

It is a happy thing that modern Persian rugs have started to copy some of the ancient garden designs of the old ones. Look in the window of an oriental-rug store, and you may see a Persian garden.

camellias

The season of camellia shows is upon us. There are over one hundred camellia societies in the United States, and each and every one puts on a beautiful annual show for the public to see. If you have never participated in putting on a flower show you cannot possibly imagine how much organizing and hard work is involved. Dozens of camellia lovers on numerous committees work for months to stage the beautiful shows for us to enjoy.

Camellias were cultivated and adored by the Chinese as far back as the ninth century. Along with the tree peony, the chrysanthemum, the lotus, and the plum blossom, they are represented on porcelain, on scrolls and panels, and in the paintings of many centuries.

The reticulata camellias seem to have especially caught their fancy. Down through the centuries, many different kinds of reticulatas were developed, entirely from bud sports, according to some authorities. If this is true, then the reticulata camellias in China are just pieces of the original trees that go back into the ninth century and are some of the very oldest of living things on earth. In modern times, of course, the reticulatas, with their upright, airy blossoms, have been crossed with many other species. Since they are susceptible to cold, the blood of cold-hardy kinds has been bred into them to develop hardy varieties.

Richard Rawes, captain of a ship of the East India Company, in 1820 brought home to England the first *Camellia reticulata* for his friend T. C. Palmer. The flowers created a real sensation among English flower lovers. They began to grow them in their greenhouses and to cherish the plants and study them. More plants were imported by John Damper Parks for the Royal Horticultural Society, and the plants of both introductions were called 'Captain Rawes' reticulatas.

The 'Captain Rawes' camellia was a single, but it was no time at all until English gardeners had the handsome double form. In 1924, the famous plant collector, George Forrest, sent plants and seeds of the wild reticulata home to England from Yunnan Province in China. These plants turned out to be vigorous types that launched the reticulatas on their present popular career.

We in America did not get excited about camellias until the 1920s. After that time, camellia fever spread very fast, mainly because American men took the camellia as one of their favorite flowers. The cult spread across the South the way it had done on the West Coast. Today the practice of "gibbing" flowers with a chemical to make them grow twice as big as normal and open sooner than their natural season is very popular. In the shows, these giant flowers compete with each other in the "gibbed" sections. Some of them are formidable!

flowering olives

The flowering olives (*Osmanthus*) are some of our choicest big evergreen shrubs. Gardens in the southern low country have always been famous for their "sweet olive" bushes, which bloom in late fall even before the camellias. For a long time people thought they would not stand the winters in the hills and mountains, but gradually, it became apparent that they were hardy enough for the "up country." Up in the hills, even in windy and exposed places, only the coldest snaps brown the leaves.

Flowering olives are not trees like the true olive (*Olea europaea*). All of the osmanthuses except our native *O. americanus* are from China and Japan. *Fragrans*, our "sweet olive," was introduced to England in 1771 and soon found its way to this country. Although we usually think of it as blooming from late fall throughout the winter, it actually is hardly ever without its tiny fragrant flowers except in summer and early fall.

Here and there over the South, there are splendid bushes of the wonderful golden- or orange-flowered variety. Inez Conger, one of the best gardeners in northern Louisiana, has long had big specimens of this wonderful plant on her place at Arcadia, and there is a big specimen in the Sarah P. Duke Gardens in Durham, North Carolina. The tiny flowers are borne in great quantities and sweeten the air in a whole neighborhood. One can sometimes find this relatively rare plant in the container nurseries under the species name *aurantiacus*.

In 1856, Thomas Lobb, an English nurseryman, introduced from Japan a flowering olive that turned out to be hardier to cold weather than *O. fragrans*. It was such a fine plant that the Royal Horticultural Society gave it a First Class certificate three years later. The new shrub combined holly-like leaves with spineless ones, and the tiny white flowers were borne in great masses under the foliage in autumn. This one was given the Latin name *aquifolium* (also *ilicifolius* in catalogues.) In modern catalogues we can find varieties with golden leaves, silver leaves, or white-margined leaves.

Both Thomas Lobb, in 1856, and Robert Fortune, the great plant explorer, in 1862, introduced a still more exciting flowering olive to England. This one is now one of our most popular fragrant evergreen shrubs here in the southern United States. It is a hybrid between *fragrans* and *aquifolium*, and it was named *O. fortunei* in Robert Fortune's honor.

Fortune's olive has grown to tremendous proportions all over our South. There are giant specimens on the campus of the University of North Carolina at Chapel Hill that are fifteen to twenty feet across. In autumn, they fill the whole campus with their fragrance. Hedges of this olive have become very popular everywhere. They should not be held back to less than ten feet across and ten to fifteen high, however; otherwise they will get sick. There are several beautiful variegated forms of Fortune's olive today, some with silver and some with gold markings.

Another splendid osmanthus called 'San Jose' is a very upright bush for narrow, tall screens, flowering early and profusely, usually beginning in September. In addition to all these olives, there are some others not often seen here. *O. delavayi* is a small-leaved, very tender, choice species, and *O. armatus* has thick leaves with stiff spines and makes a very protective hedge against all comers.

pinks, old and new

What has happened to the old-fashioned pinks our grandmothers used to grow as edgers to their flower borders? If we cannot grow carnations except in the cooler parts of the South, we can surely grow pinks. They are easily raised from seed and bloom in late spring or summer from an early spring sowing. Here in the South, even the annual pinks may live for several years like perennials. Both the true perennial pinks and the annuals can be propagated by taking off side shoots in early fall and simply sticking them in the ground. They will root very quickly and provide new plants for next year's blooming.

The pinks with silvery foliage have always made splendid borders for beds of flowers where there is good drainage. They contrast with the green perennials and annuals and show off the other flowers like a silver frame. In a short time, they will make big mats of silvery foliage that smother most of the weeds. At Edwards Gardens in Toronto I saw a beautiful show of the plain or solid-color varieties alternating with mixed colors along the front of a border. Like the carnation, pinks were grown in monastery gardens for over a thousand years. Most of them smell of cloves, and picking one to smell is irresistible.

Good garden soil with a little lime is what they need. They do like sunshine, but half-shade will suffice for most kinds. Both annual and perennial types want the same kind of treatment.

There has been a renaissance in pinks lately. In England, Graham Thomas and other perennials lovers have been searching out the old, old named pinks and carnations. The late Constance Spry, a flower decorator who lectured here back in the thirties, used to go to the flower market in the Hay Market in London in search of old flowers. She would pay the flower ladies to propagate them so they could then sell the flowers to her for her famous shop in Audley Street. During World War II I visited her there one morning after a particularly bomb-filled night, and we reminisced about her visit to the South.

Current seed catalogues carry any number of old as well as new pinks. Some of them are fringed, with a light, airy look. Several have won All-America awards. Look in the indexes; there are as many as eight different kinds of pinks scattered through the pages of some catalogues.

native hollies

Only a few plant lovers, gardeners, and nurserymen paid much attention to any of our wild American hollies except the "typical" American holly (*Ilex opaca*) fifty years ago. Then an old seed and plant store in New Orleans planted a big hedge of yaupon (*I. vomitoria*) in front of their store, a hedge that grew more beautiful year by year. On my second lecture visit to Shreveport in the thirties, I spoke at the State Exhibition Building, a unique round structure. Leading up to the building, there is a walk with the most magnificent hedge of yaupon imaginable. Boxwood could never stand up to the heat and the alternate droughts and tornadic rains of Shreveport, but this yaupon from the coast thrives on such weather. On all my subsequent visits to Shreveport, I have insisted upon visiting this magnificent hedge. If you go there, be sure to see it. Not long after the thirties people began to see how handsome yaupon was, and it began to show up in southern landscapes.

The trouble with yaupon had been that the bushes grew too fast. It needed pruning several times a year—something we lazy southerners do not want to do. This problem was eliminated by old Mr. Jennings, in Louisiana, when he discovered the dwarf yaupon "down on the Gulf."

Dwarf yaupon—"Like most dwarf plants, this fine-leaved beauty is really just a slow grower."

Like most dwarf plants, this fine-leaved beauty is really just a slow grower. It strongly resembles the English boxwood (*Buxus sempervirens*) that Americans dote on, and which does not like the hotter parts of the South.

The early explorers of the South found the Indians making a tea out of fermented and dried yaupon leaves. Some of the coastal Indians also had an annual ceremony at which they drank hot yaupon tea made from the green leaves.

Another native holly is the dahoon (*I. cassine*) that inhabits the coastal plains. This primarily narrow-leaved species is best known to gardeners through its hybrids 'East Palatka', 'Hume No. 1', and the splendid and popular 'Hume No. 2'. Both 'Humes' were collected by the late, distinguished Harold Hume and introduced by the old Glen Saint Mary Nursery in Florida.

An even more elegant native holly than the dahoon or yaupon is the fine-foliaged myrtle-leaf holly (*I. cassine myrtifolia*). This species will grow right out in the water—an amazing thing for a holly to do. Around some of the coastal lakes and shallow ponds, these shapely hollies look like Christmas trees standing on a mirror of black water. Fortunately, these refined little evergreen trees will grow on dry land as well as in the water. One seldom finds them offered in nursery catalogues, but the holly called 'Foster' (*I. × attenuata* 'Fosteri') looks so much like myrtle-leaf and is normally so much denser that it makes a fine substitute.

The female bushes of our common deciduous holly (*I. decidua*) put on such a grand show of berries that we have begun to pay it some attention, even though it is not evergreen. Traveling over the southern states, one can see many variations in the color of its berries. In Mississippi they are often a real orange instead of red. Another nonevergreen holly is the colorful "black alder," not an alder at all, but a true holly (*I. verticillata*), which usually grows in wettish places. This one is the earliest native holly to color up in autumn. It is always a sign that autumn has begun when "black alder" turns red. For a wet spot it is just the thing.

aucubas, the great shade lovers

Nothing loves the shade more than aucubas. If you have a dark corner where nothing else will survive, aucubas will probably thrive there. Some of the variegated, striped or blotched, types can lighten up almost any dull spot. There are many leaf types among the green aucubas: large, small, long and narrow, even lacy types.

Aucubas are male and female on separate bushes, so if you want some berries, be sure to get female plants and a male or two for pollen. Young plants are mostly grown from seed by the nurseries, except for the special named cultivars. Seedlings do not have to be much over a foot tall, however, before they reveal their sex, so you can select the berry and nonberry types in the nursery or on plant stands.

Experienced gardeners know how easy it is to root aucubas simply by cutting a piece and leaving it in a clear glass vase or container in the sun in a window. The plants will grow from six inches to a foot per year. They will take pruning, but they will not like being kept down below two or three feet in height. They can withstand extremely low temperatures, as witness their presence in cold New York City. In the South they will scald in the sun and turn black. For so fine a shade lover to be planted in the sun is a genuine shame!

Aucubas were sent to England as early as 1783, but, as the single plant sent was a female, there were no berries until male plants were sent sometime between 1856 and 1866. Almost a century passed before the English saw how beautiful the big berries are!

The coal smoke and the grime of London before the clean-air laws were very hard on plants. Since aucubas resisted both with no trouble, these cheerful plants became very popular in the city—so much so that costermongers sold them from their barrows in the streets. Although they are not as plentiful there as they were fifty years ago when people overdid them, groups of the yellow-variegated types look mighty good in dark corners in the dead of the London winter.

mediterranean flowers

The Mediterranean Basin from Gibraltar to Israel is full of flowers that like our gardening conditions here in the South. We should grow more of these plants from the hot countries like North Africa, Spain, southern Italy, Greece, Turkey, Israel, and the rest of the Middle East.

A set of books so rare that only one set of them had changed hands in forty years came into my hands in 1946. In three enormous volumes, the authors, Jordan and Fourreau, two Frenchmen, illustrated in color many of the flowers of the countries around the Mediterranean. The work, *Icones ad floram Europae*, was planned to continue and illustrate all the flora of Europe, but the project was never completed. Luckily for me, it started with plants from southern France, Spain, Morocco, Algeria, Italy, and Greece. Such a work is an eternal inspiration to a southern gardener and botanist, because to see these plants in color and in so many, many different natural varieties spurs one on to get them and grow them here in the southern states.

Page after page of wild daffodils, the ancestors of our modern ones, show how the genus *Narcissus* can vary. In southern Spain and Portugal, there are many little hoop-petticoat daffodils, some of which are white and bloom in late fall and winter. Here in the South we have hardly begun to be conscious of these small flowers. We have had a small yellow one (*N. bulbocodium conspicuus*) for a hundred years, but the citron yellow species (*N. romieuxii*) that flowers in January and February is a more recent arrival.

The little Spanish and Portugese daffodils grow well and multiply here in the hot South. The tiny trumpet, *Narcissus asturiensis* (*N. minimus*) grows and blooms in January or February. It is beginning to appear in early daffodil shows. Besides this one, there are ten or more of these gems now in some bulb catalogues. Jan de Graaff used to grow them in Oregon, but he told me that he had given up listing them a long time ago. Thank heaven, some West Coast bulb dealers offer them today.

Cyclamens, sternbergias, chionodoxas, hyacinths of all kinds, tulips, santolina, Italian arum, tamarix trees, lavender, and rosemary all come from hot countries like ours. One of the most beautiful trees in the Mediterranean is the strawberry tree, *Arbutus unedo*, an evergreen that has flowers and fruits all at the same time. The flowers look like white heather bells. The fruit resembles the strawberry but is not edible that I know of.

Perhaps the most accommodating of all bulbous plants, *Scilla peruviana*, comes from the North African countries. This remarkable bulb grows and flourishes in the waddies of Morocco in the mud. It does equally well up on the hot, dry Rock of Gibraltar. Its name came from the little boat in which it arrived in England and has nothing to do with Peru! The great French botanist Clusius is said to have traveled all the way across to England to see the new plants brought home in the bark *Peru*.

winter care of trees

Trees are too valuable to be neglected. Winter ice and sleet storms will get them if they are not kept in shape to stand up to the weight of ice. This is the time to look over every single tree on your premises and have the proper pruning and shaping done by professional tree surgeons —not by untrained people. If you do not do it, nature may destroy your trees. We are so accustomed to their presence that we fail to look for defects such as rot where limbs were pruned, starvation, and improper shaping.

In a grove of trees, some may grow to be lopsided—heavier on one side than on the other. These specimens may well succumb to the weight of ice or sleet. Tree surgeons can balance them by the removal of some of the limbs on the heavy side. This will usually save the tree when it is weighted with ice. Along streets, too, where the limbs have been shorn away by electric linesmen, the trees may collapse under the stress of hurricanes and storms.

Where limbs have been removed, all too often an excessively long stub is left that will rot and carry the decay down into the main trunk of the tree. Eventually this condition will be responsible for its demise. It does not happen quickly, so we do not notice it until it is too far gone to be remedied. When a limb is removed, the cut should be made just outside the wrinkles where the limb joins the main trunk.

Especially where trees are struggling along to survive in limited space and poor soil, they simply must be fed regularly. This is where people err most grievously! We do take our forests and our shade trees for granted. They will survive for a few years on what their roots can find in the soil, but when the food is not there, they will surely die of starvation. Since we rake up all the twigs and leaves every year, a shade tree cannot build up the soil underneath its branches as it does in the wild.

Trees in special shapes like the weeping cherries need support after they have developed large branching trunks. The weight of ice on the innumerable little weeping branches will bring down the trunks if they are not supported individually. The same supports can be used over again each winter and can be stored away for the summer when spring comes. A fine old specimen is well worth this trouble. The catch is to remember the supports before the ice comes around.

It is surprising how many weeping cherries one sees with the main trunk asserting itself to the detriment of the weeping branches. If you do not prune away the growth from the straight trunk on which the weeping parts have been grafted or budded, sooner or later the upright growths will develop into a large upright tree, and the weepers will die out.

black-berried hollies

We are so accustomed to the red berries on American, English, and Chinese hollies that we do not realize there are also hollies with black berries. In the coastal plain from Nova Scotia to Florida and Texas, our big gallberry (*Ilex coriacea*) grows in small thickets. The small gallberry, called inkberry (*I. glabra*), is also native to the coastal plain from Virginia southward. Both of these have black berries that are, indeed, as bitter as gall. Try one!

The handsome, black-fruited Japanese holly (*I. crenata*) hardly existed in southern gardens before World War I. Today, it is one of our most valuable fine-leaved evergreens. It will grow in many places where boxwood is not at all happy. Since some varieties can withstand temperatures as low as eighteen degrees below zero, gardeners grow it as far north as Boston.

Plant collectors visiting Japan have been astonished to see old hedges of Japanese holly so thick and strong that a small child could walk over their tops. Any plant so accommodating, so thick with evergreen leaves, and so tough was bound to appear in our gardens. It certainly was welcome here in the South and has become one of the most popular elements of southern landscapes.

When raised from seed this holly has given rise to many different varieties. Some of these are tall, upright plants, graceful as specimens or splendid when planted close together as hedges. Here and there, one sees a beautiful specimen standing by itself in a foundation planting. This upright type has beautiful yellow twigs that give a total effect of a delightfully "different" yellow green.

A large variety called 'Rotundifolia' by some nurseries, if unpruned, makes huge, rounded, slightly flat mounds of green. The oldest ones here in the South must be by now twelve to fourteen feet across! In most plantings, these handsome shrubs have unfortunately been pruned into ball shapes.

One of the most popular varieties is called 'Convexa' because of the cup-shaped leaves. This one is fairly upright and grows up in a hurry. 'Convexa' needs a little pruning, however, if you wish to keep it dense, because it tends to grow into a big, open bush if left to its own pattern of growth.

Rare in southern gardens is the tiny-leaved upright 'Microphylla'. For some reason, nurseries did not like it and stopped propagating it. There is, however, no more exquisite fine-leaved upright screen for very narrow places.

It took nurseries a long time to get enough of the variety 'Helleri' on the market to satisfy the public. 'Helleri' makes handsome mounds of fine foliage that are extremely effective in the foreground of plantings. It should be given plenty of space, however, for the specimens will attain six feet across in time. Wherever a substitute for boxwood is needed, the more upright 'Stokes' should be planted.

If you wish to make a bonsai, you cannot find a more suitable plant than the very dwarf 'Mariesii', collected by C. Maries in 1879 for Messrs. Veitch, the famous London nurserymen. There are many new Japanese hollies coming into nurseries today—all of them excellent plants.

climbing roses

With the days already getting perceptibly longer, we had better get at some of the tasks of late January. One of these is the pruning of climbing roses. If you have a long climber on the house or on a trellis, the very best thing to do is to take it completely off the support before you try to prune it. You may have to lighten the mass of twigs and canes some before you let the whole thing down. Otherwise the weight may damage the larger canes by bending them too much. After the climber is down, it is easiest to begin at the ground with your pruning. Select to be saved the youngest canes and some of the older ones that are healthy looking and then begin the process of pruning by following the ones you are eliminating through the tangle and cutting them out bit by bit. Whatever you do, do not yank and pull long pieces out because you will bruise and scar the rose and these places will be subject to disease later on. It is no trouble at all to trim a rose if you will simply cut out little foot-long pieces.

If you are a rose fan, you will know that the old wood on 'Dr. Van

Fleet', that long-climbing, light pink rose and its everblooming form called 'New Dawn' will bloom on and on for years without pruning. The same is true of 'Silver Moon'. As long as they do not get completely out of hand, let them go. They will cover a house if the house is strong enough to hold them up!

We southerners ought to plant 'Maréchal Niel' more often, even if it does not always do too well. If it does not succeed in one place, then try it in another, for there is still not a more beautiful yellow climber for the southern states. Just think, it was introduced by Fradel back in 1864! One of its ancestors was a rose raised in Charleston, South Carolina, in 1810 by a gentleman named Champney. Mr. Champney's rose was called 'Champney's Pink Cluster' and combined the virtues of the China rose with those of the musk rose. Another Charlestonian, the French nurseryman, Philippe Noisette, raised a second rose from the Champney rose and sent it to his brother in Paris in 1814. French nurserymen sold the new Noisette rose and also used it in their breeding of new varieties. In this country, it was called 'Old Blush (French) Noisette Rose'. The French artist, Redouté, painted it in 1821 in his great book *Les Roses*, the most beautiful book on roses ever published. In bookstores today, there are several books on Redouté's roses with reproductions in color of his famous engravings.

During the time of Napoleon III Maréchal Niel was secretary of state. One day, on a tour of inspection of French fortresses, he was at Avignon. The banquet hall where he was being entertained was filled with beautiful yellow roses. The maréchal, who was a rose lover, sent for the local florist who had discovered the rose and congratulated him on it. Whereupon the florist said that he would name the rose 'Madame la Maréchale' in honor of the maréchal's wife. The fact that the maréchal was a bachelor saved us from having this long French name for our 'Maréchal Niel'! Once this rose gets started, it will grow to great size here in the South. Visiting Jerry Powers in Houston recently, I looked out his kitchen window and saw a 'Maréchal Niel' growing so far along a fence that I had to go outdoors to see all of it. Such fragrance! The lovely yellow buds stand up straight and the open flowers pout coyly on their stems. In Spain, there is a specimen ten inches in diameter at the base! It is growing at Granada in the Gardens of the Alhambra. The famous and beloved rosarian and rose breeder Dr. Nicolas, who visited this rose and identified it in 1930, said that his French friend, the rose breeder Dot, confirmed his identification.

february

winter flowers

The hardiness of tiny crocuses and cyclamens is wonderful. How do these little blossoms stand up to repeated drops in the temperature? The foliage of some beautiful plants like the Italian arum (*Arum italicum*) and the delicate-looking poet's laurel (*Danae racemosa*) can do the same.

The big-leaved "sweet ivy" (*Hedera colchica*) is only beautified by cold winds. Down in my valley in a real frost pocket, sweet ivy usually takes the cold and stays perfectly green, but on a wall exposed to the northwest wind, its big, thick leaves turn a beautiful purple except for a little edge of green. The Europeans consider this the most beautiful of ivies. It grows all over Asia Minor and up into the Caucasus. Here in the South, it will take over the woods and all the trees if allowed to.

After a night in the low teens the sun came out the other day, and the amazing little orange flowers of *Crocus ancyrensis* 'Golden Bunch' brightened up one of my hillsides where it had been interplanted with some Italian arums. The little flowers are tiny round bowls of gold and are the feature of January and February anywhere they grow.

Over on another slope, the winter sunshine had opened up the blue form of *C. chrysanthus*—the one called 'Blue Butterfly'. How can any wild yellow or orange crocus with purple stripes give rise to so many, many variations? The English love crocuses—as we southerners will learn to love them too, I am sure, when we begin to grow them more.

E. A. Bowles, who wrote three books about his garden, selected numerous seedlings of this crocus, ranging all the way from gold to blue! He showed these delightful winter flowers at the winter shows of the Royal Horticultural Society in London and won many honors with them. Today, we can buy these crocuses from American bulb dealers in the autumn with our daffodils.

Our southern winters are much like those in England. Mr. Bowles' crocuses flower here at about the same time they do in England and will eventually become one of the real features of our winter gardens. For a long time, we did not find anything but the common spring crocuses in our stores and catalogues, but the fall and early spring types are there now—why are we so reluctant to try anything new!

By the end of January, a great many different winter crocuses have come and gone. Mr. Bowles' named varieties of *C. chrysanthus* do make the biggest show of all the winter groups. In warm southern gardens, they too have come and gone by the end of January. When next year's fall bulb catalogues from Holland appear, look for 'Advance' (golden yellow), 'Blue Beauty', 'Blue Throat', 'Blue Bonnet', 'Blue Butterfly', 'Blue Giant', 'Blue Pearl', 'Blue Peter', 'Bullfinch' (cream, feathered with crimson purple), 'E. A. Bowles' (butter yellow), 'Gypsy Girl' (yellow and chocolate), 'Goldilocks' (golden yellow, feathered with bronze), 'Ladykiller' (white and deep mauve; why does mauve get the ladies!), 'Marion' (deep purple stripes; very early), 'Snow Bunting' (white with featherings; very popular), 'Sultan' (mahogany and white), 'Warley White' (cream and purple), and 'Zwanenburg' (spectacular, large flowers of deep orange with mahogany outside).

winter cold

Even this cold winter has not subdued everything in the garden. A tough little sternbergia has been in bloom—one flower after another—in my woodsy garden since Christmas. The winter-flowering crocuses have certainly been slowed down this year, but even they are now in full bloom. Then the little winter cyclamens from the Turkish mountains discovered how long the days were and started to bloom last week. The cold has not frightened the winter jasmine too much; it has been opening a few flowers on the rare warm days.

My friend Deeda Sessoms always keeps a fresh flower arrangement in a bank in Chapel Hill. Several weeks back, she had camellias, winter jasmine, evergreen leaves and berries, and wintersweet in her arrangement. How cheerful to see out-of-door flowers every time one goes to the bank!

What we call wintersweet in the South has been given a number of names by botanists. It used to be called *Meratia praecox*. Before that, it was called *Calycanthus praecox*. Today, the botanists are calling it *Chimonanthus praecox*, and that is what you will have to look for in books and catalogues. At least they have not changed the *praecox* part of its official name. *Praecox* means precocious, applicable in this case because this winter flower blooms early in the season. Translated, the full name means early snowflower. But whatever name you may choose, wintersweet is one of the real winter bloomers. Any time after the end of November, it may begin to open its strange little flowers that resemble the blossoms of sweet shrub (*Calycanthus floridus*) to which it is closely akin. Our grandmothers had wintersweet in their gardens. Back in the thirties gardeners rediscovered it, and many people planted it. Once you have a bush you will never wish to be without the little sweet flowers in the toughest winter weeks.

The tiny golden flowers of my *Crocus aureus* started to open a week ago in spite of nights down to ten degrees! Then, several days ago, the violet form of *C. chrysanthus* startled me. Once you have these real winter crocuses, the common Dutch crocuses will not please you as much because they are really late!

Most of us have sweet-breath-of-spring (*Lonicera fragrantissima*) in our gardens somewhere. It has been reluctant to bloom very much so far this year. Robert Fortune, that indefatigable plant hunter, introduced this sweet bush honeysuckle from China in 1845 along with another fragrant honeysuckle, but *fragrantissima* has always been the popular one, and old gardens everywhere below Mason and Dixon's line have enormous bushes of it. Not at all showy, the tiny flowers begin to spread their fragrance in winter, after every cold snap. The leaves of this honeysuckle are only semievergreen and the bushes are open and loose. Neverthless, walks were bordered with it, and walls of its light green leaves and fragrant flowers grew up to twelve feet along paths and walks of camellia gardens. Along with sweet olive, it bespeaks the South in winter.

christmas roses and lenten roses

Lenten Roses (*Helleborus orientalis*) began to come alive way back when the Christmas Roses (*H. niger*) were in bloom in gardens where they thrive. These two fascinating winter perennials are always a joy, even here in the South where we have camellias in bloom in the winter. Along with the winter iris, wintersweet, sweet-breath-of-spring, winter jasmine, and Bongoume apricot, they provide us with excitement and a lot to talk about from December to March. The variation in time of bloom, from year to year, of Christmas Roses seems to depend upon moisture conditions and the weather. After dry times, they may be a little late, but sometimes they bloom as early as before Christmas.

Do not be impatient if these plants get off to a slow start in your yard or garden. They just do not move very fast. Both of them like a soil with a clay base. If you plant them in sandy soils, take care that they never become really dry.

The most common site for both of these hellebores is on the north side of the house up close to the foundations. If bad gutters do not continually drown them, they seem to like this position. Lime from the mortar in the bricks of the foundation is to their liking, and you could hardly find a cooler spot anywhere. Some of the best hellebores are to be found, too, in shady camellia gardens over the South. The beautiful evergreen foliage makes a splendid ground cover.

More and more kinds of Christmas Roses and Lenten Roses are coming into this country through the novelty nurseries. In England, there are numerous purple, light yellow, white, and green varieties that are highly prized during the dark winter months. These plants have always fascinated Europeans because of their winter flowering and abundant foliage.

hardy annuals

It is time to sow the seeds of the hardy annuals if you did not plant any back in September or October. The plants that will come from seeds sown now will rarely be as big as the autumn-sown ones and will produce later-flowering plants, too, but they will be good enough to bloom from mid-spring up into hot weather. One advantage of an early spring sowing is the avoidance of the winterkill that is sometimes a result of autumn seeding.

Larkspur is so sophisticated now that you can hardly tell some of it from delphinium, though it will not be as tall. Get seeds of some of the separate colors and some of the double form. Snapdragons do not mind the cool weather and will go on in the heat and make fine plants to bloom all summer. They are really perennials. Clarkia is a beautiful delicate annual, but the sudden heat usually finishes it off quickly. If you grow it, put it where it will get some shade for part of the day and do not ever let it suffer for lack of water.

The old-fashioned love-in-a-mist (*Nigella damascena*) is a superb annual that people are discovering again. The fine foliage would be worthwhile even if the plants never bloomed. At the time the old-fashioned roses are in bloom, this old annual produces small light blue, white, or pink flowers amongst its fuzzy green foliage.

Johnny-jump-ups (*Viola tricolor*) are dear to the hearts of many gardeners. They will literally jump up and grow almost anywhere—in poor soil, especially. Maybe they do not actually prefer poor soil, but they do seem to grow where nothing else will. Once you have even a few, you will always be blessed with these charming little things. They are easily hoed out where you do not want them. In some yards I saw last summer, there were big patches of a bright violet one which were delightful.

It was a lucky day for us when Chinese forget-me-nots (*Cynoglossum amabile*) came to our gardens. These wonderful flowers bring more near-blue into southern gardens than almost anything one can grow. They will come up and start at any time of the year and remain with you if you let them seed themselves from year to year.

To get the most out of the hardy annuals, plant them in pots in a cold frame. There need be no heat at all to encourage them to grow and try to catch up to the fall-sown ones, and the advantage of little potted or flat-raised plants over plants from scattered seed is that you can tuck them into exactly the places where they will be the most effective in the garden.

daffodils

Daffodils, in one form or another, have been favorite flowers all the way back to the early Egyptians, who put them in tombs with the dead. Ovid thought the name *Narcissus* was associated with the youth who admired his reflection in a fountain in the spring and was turned into a flower. Pliny, however, thought the name came from the word *narkē*, because of the flower's narcotic perfume. Our popular name for this large group of bulbs may well be a corruption of the word *asphodel*. Whatever the derivation, and whatever you may call your favorites, they are all different kinds of daffodil in English and all belong to the Latin genus *Narcissus*.

All the nations around the Mediterranean have loved the many kinds of daffodils native there. The Europeans took them into their colder countries and cultivated them. In modern times, the Dutch and the English, especially, have cherished daffodils and developed many varieties. We know that they were cultivated as early as 1570 and that they were popular in Queen Elizabeth's time. Old John Gerard tells us in his *Herbal* of 1596 that the double form of *N. polyanthus* was sent from Constantinople "to the Right Hon. the Lord Treasurer among other bulbed flowers."

John Parkinson's big garden book of 1629 has six big folio plates showing thirty-seven varieties of daffodils. The title of this, perhaps the most exciting garden book ever published, is *Paradisi in Sole, Paradisus Terrestris*. The title is a play on words—a popular convention in the author's day—and might be translated roughly "gardens (or parks) in the sun, heaven on earth." Botany was a little mixed up in those days, however, and some of Parkinson's daffodils are now known to be something else.

Many of the very old daffodils are growing today in old gardens over the South, and gardeners are beginning to really appreciate these tough old bulbs. The ground temperature and climate of the South are so much like those around the Mediterranean, home of the whole genus, that they settle down in our gardens to stay.

By 1875, when F. W. Burbidge published his beautifully illustrated book, *The Narcissus, Its History and Culture*, there were over three hundred and fifty species and varieties for him to discuss. The forty-eight color plates are a sure guide to the identification of our old daffodils. In my copy of this treasury, someone, apparently Burbidge himself, has drawn and then painted with water colors, on the pages facing the plates, a number of delightful daffodils not included in the book. They are more beautifully executed than the plates themselves.

We now have 279 pages of names alone in the *Classified List and International Register of Daffodil Names*, published by the Royal Horticultural Society in London.

winter daffodils

By the time the little early trumpets open in southern gardens, many of the tiny winter-blooming daffodils have bloomed and gone. Some of them flower as early as December in the gardens of daffodil enthusiasts. In the past the public never paid much attention to any daffodils except the ordinary kinds, but lately, gardeners are beginning to look for small plants to enjoy in very small gardens.

All around the Mediterranean there are small kinds of wild narcissus which flower in autumn and winter. One of them (*N. viridiflorus*), with an exceedingly sweet green flower, blooms in the autumn months. Another (*N. serotinus*), which bloomed for me in September, is so small it is hardly visible. Unfortunately its genetic make-up is not one which will cross with any other variety, so we cannot develop a race of little fall-flowering daffodils from it. By Thanksgiving, of course, the paper-whites bloom all across the southern states from upper Louisiana through the coastal plains to Norfolk. Even up in the hill country above the coastal plain the snow-white hoop-petticoat from Spain and Algeria has been blooming in December for years in some southern gardens. This one is the first of the winter-flowering daffodils. In catalogues, it is *Narcissus bulbocodium monophyllus*. *Monophyllus* means that it has only one leaf.

Another winter treasure that is happy above the coastal plain and flowers during the first weeks of January in protected spots is the hoop-petticoat *N. b. romieuxii*. It sends up its wiry little leaves and flower stems and opens up a lemon yellow flower no bigger across than a nickel. The flowers are amazingly frost resistant. I have had them put their heads back up after a night in the twenties! They come from the bleak Atlas Mountains of North Africa and can really take it.

Some time later in January or early February, the tiniest of all trumpet daffodils, *N. asturiensis*, from Asturia in Spain sounds its little horn. The foliage is not more than two or three inches high, and the trumpet less than half an inch long. This one draws all the attention in a winter flower show.

There are still other delightful varieties of winter daffodils. You can read about them in Elizabeth Lawrence's book *The Little Bulbs*. She has something about them, too, in her *A Southern Garden*. Another source of information is Alec Gray's *Miniature Daffodils*. The West Coast bulb nurseries like Grant Mitsch of Canby, Oregon 97013, are good sources for bulbs in this country.

snowdrops and snowflakes

Snowdrops are so rare in southern gardens that most gardeners have seen very few of them. They are beloved by English gardeners, whose literature and poetry are full of the praises of these white winter flowers.

Many serious gardeners have ordered and planted the snowdrop bulbs only to have them flower, if at all, only once and then play out and disappear. Now the snowdrop fanciers tell us that the time to transplant these little finickies is right after they bloom and with the green leaves still on them! Well, we shall all have to try, because once you have seen a patch of snowdrops in bloom in the middle of the winter, you will never quite get over it. How could anything have such a power over plant lovers!

Believe it or not, there are a few gardens in the South in woodsy areas where snowdrops have been established and are spreading. There is a garden in Atlanta where I was enchanted to see the little flowers all over the woods in with the azaleas. This species certainly likes woods mold. In Old Salem, North Carolina, last year, I was amazed to see big healthy clumps of one of the bigger species growing right beside a driveway. They were so lusty that I was all but sure they were snowflakes instead of snowdrops. Two weeks ago, I received pressed flowers from the garden owner, Flora Ann Bynum, and they are indeed snowdrops!

Back in the thirties, many of us in the South tried out all sorts of "new" bulbs and alpine plants and compared notes on them. Of course, not many of the true alpine rockery plants survived, but some kinds of snowdrops did. They were the wild ones from the hotter parts of the Mediterranean. So we shall gradually learn which kinds we can grow permanently here in the South in the hills and mountains.

Woodsy soil and some bone meal seem to be the chief needs of snowdrops. In soil without leaf mold and in hot, very dry places, they do not seem to make it. Not too many kinds are offered in American catalogues. We shall simply have to buy what is available and try our luck. To learn more about them, read Elizabeth Lawrence's *The Little Bulbs*.

The common snowflakes of old gardens all over the South are different from snowdrops. While they are akin, snowdrops are *Galanthus* and snowflakes are *Leucojum*. The long stems of snowflakes—twelve to fifteen inches—are giants compared to those of snowdrops. Most of our snowflakes are the common "summer" kind, though they actually bloom here in the spring, and the named variety called 'Gravetye Giant' is more floriferous by far than the common old one. Perhaps the most useful thing about snowflakes is that they will grow in low, wettish places where few bulbs would survive. You can see them in masses in my favorite Cypress Garden near Charleston, where I was once adviser. There they grow along the water's edge and are a little taller than the atamasco lilies.

hedges and screens

In these days when people are living on smaller and smaller plots of land, hedges and screens have become more important. In residential areas, screens of plants at the property line can block the view of one house from the other and preserve a lot of privacy. During the summer heat, hedges are preferable to tight fences in most cases because fences do not allow the air to flow through. Such screens need not be all of one variety of tree or shrub but can comprise several different kinds, although preferably all evergreens.

On big properties, magnolias and hollies enrich the winter landscape. They need plenty of room to grow into mature trees, however. Next in size come the photinias, the evergreen privets, elaeagnus—to climb into trees if you like—then *Camellia sasanqua* and *C. japonica*. All of these can be made into a big screen all the way around big properties. Various combinations of them give interesting variety.

Two of our finest native plants for hedges are dwarf varieties of yaupon (*Ilex vomitoria*) and wax myrtle (*Myrica cerifera*). The excellent dwarf yaupon can be made into gorgeous, tight, boxwood-like hedges. It does not have the fragrance of boxwood, but neither is it subject to the pests and troubles of that traditional hedge that are especially bothersome in areas where boxwood is not happy. Wax myrtle is a different shade of green from most of our broadleaf evergreens. Its olive green color is strongly reminiscent of Italian gardens and their olive trees— also of the green Italian marble. It can be kept fairly small—even down to three to five feet with good pruning. If it gets too big and has not been pruned, it can still be reduced with severe pruning and will come out and fatten up. Wax myrtle is a fire plant. It is able to come back from its roots after a forest fire. Both it and dwarf yaupon stand up well to droughts, a great point in their favor.

Where a completely protective hedge is needed, the two evergreen barberries are effective. Julian's barberry (*Berberis julianae*) is somewhat more rounded in form than the Sargent barberry (*B. sargentiana*), which is slightly upright in stature and suited to narrow places. Dogs and cats will not go through these hedges, but "Brer Rabbit" sometimes does.

Where hedges pass underneath trees and shrubs, they must compete for nutrients. Feed the hedge more where it is in such competition. Otherwise it will starve and become spindly. Here in the South, we are blessed with many, many good hedge plants to choose from.

starving plants

This is the time of the year, while the trees are bare, when it is easy to see what plants are starving in your garden or yard. Undernourished broadleaf evergreens are yellow green instead of a good, healthy, deep green. Conifers are thin looking with sparse needles and little dead tips.

The competition among plants grown as close together as we like to see them in our landscapes makes it necessary to fertilize everything in yard and garden once a year, or even more often. Shade trees with their deep roots can better survive, if the subsoil is good, than shrubs with their shallower root systems. But the subsoil is not rich enough in most places for even the shade trees to grow well without a feeding at least every other year.

Trees and shrubs should be fed right now just before growth starts and again in the fall. A lot of fertilizer put on after growth stops in midsummer may run away in big rains so it is best to inject it into the soil several inches by the hole-punching method. Arboriculturists have recently decided that an autumn feeding is very effective.

Starving bulbs like daffodils and tulips that have stopped blooming regularly will respond remarkably to a feeding right now while the foliage is developing. The plant food will help them make bigger bulbs, some of which may then flower the next year. It is well to take them up later, replant those of blooming size in the garden, and set out the little ones in rows in the vegetable garden to grow on a season or so.

Old clumps of perennials are better off divided if they have stopped flowering. This does not apply to peonies, which can often be nursed back to flowering with adequate fertilizer, but it does apply especially to fast multipliers like summer phloxes, Michaelmas daisies, and shasta daisies. Replant the healthiest divisions and then fertilize them.

Since commercial fertilizer requires petroleum in its manufacture and is expensive to use, it is a sound ecological practice for every gardener to keep a compost pile going at all times. The days when we wasteful Americans threw away rich garbage in landfills is over now. Thank heaven we stopped burning leaves a few years ago. Garbage from each household and leaves from each yard will go a long way toward putting back the original fertility of the soil in our country.

Gardeners may be obliged to take what fertilizer they can get in future years and it may not come in the forms to which we have been accustomed. Bone meal and superphosphate were in short supply in the winter of 1974, for example.

cold damage to evergreens

The damage that extreme cold does to our evergreen trees and shrubs here in the South varies a great deal. Most gardeners know which evergreens are tender, but most of us grow some of the tender kinds anyway, because plants like sweet olive give us so much pleasure even if they do get nipped occasionally in the hills and mountains.

Sweet olive (*Osmanthus fragrans*) and loquat (*Eriobotrya japonica*) are known to be tender to temperatures below twenty degrees, so we plant them in protected places on the south or east sides of our houses or in protected chimney corners to avoid the cold northwest winds. Even in such places, the foliage of these and other tender evergreens may get burned, but the limbs and trunks are seldom killed. After extreme winters, it may be necessary to prune away the frozen branchlets, but the main stems will be all right and come out again. Even southern magnolias (*Magnolia grandiflora*) can be browned by gales of cold wind from the north. They will not be seriously damaged by this, however.

Underfed broadleaf evergreens do not stand up to the cold as well as those that have been properly fertilized. Ride through any town and look at the evergreens. Brown leaves after a freeze indicate starving shrubs. Japanese privet (*Ligustrum japonicum*) is the one you will see the most of. For some reason, gardeners will plant this evergreen in all kinds of horrible places and then let it starve to death. It accommodates us by growing very fast, but it takes a lot of food to make such lusty growth, and we forget to keep it fed.

The evergreen azaleas are thin leaved. When they are underfed, the foliage turns brown in a hurry with extreme weather. However, azalea lovers usually keep their favorites well nourished. Camellias are very resistant to cold because of the thickness of their foliage. It is the buds which are subject to extreme cold. There is almost no stem at all to a camellia flower—only a small layer of cells—and these stem cells freeze very easily and drop the buds to the ground.

Needle evergreens are not all immune to extreme cold. Some of the fancy colored false-cypresses (*Chamaecyparis*), for instance, will turn brown instead of the desirable violet or blue if you do not keep them fed. Without cold weather, however, the colored conifers like Waukegan juniper (*Juniperus horizontalis douglasii*) would remain green all winter and never put on the handsome blue-greens and violets that make this one so attractive.

winter damage, cold frames, pits, and hotbeds

Strange indeed was the damage to bulbs last winter. Right in the same garden, some crinums were killed and others were not. The same must have been true of many kinds of bulbs all over the South. Perhaps it was all because of the depth to which the ground froze in different spots.

Someone called me in great distress because he had lost all of his cannas. They were the new, improved variety and had been growing in the same place for years. I was sorry he had lost his plants, but the South surely will not be at any great loss if those hideous beds of old-fashioned orange and red cannas that have always grown around red brick cotton mills have gone. The new cannas are a great improvement on the old ones; they are shorter and have much larger flowers and a longer season of bloom.

We hope the sun is getting its spots back again and the winters will return to normal, but if we are to have more very cold winters, we can cover tender bulbs with a deep mulch. Gardeners in Zone 8 are accustomed to protecting ginger lilies (*Hedychium coronarium*), amaryllises, and some of the South African bulbs. Actually, we could grow a good many of the tender bulbs in our gardens if we would take the trouble to protect them in winter. The ixias are easy to grow with protection, antholyzas, babianas and other tender bulbs that do not have evergreen foliage are manageable this way, and the very tenderest ones will grow in a cold frame or in a cool greenhouse. Greenhouse owners from Norfolk to Corpus Christi grow most of the tender bulbs without any heat except in extreme weather.

Sun porches and heatless greenhouses attached to living rooms have always been popular in the South, and now we are beginning to appreciate the heat they provide. Gardeners will surely begin to discover how easy it is to grow lettuce, radishes, sweet peas, and many other plants in heatless sun porches and greenhouses.

Our grandmothers grew an unbelievable number of plants in cold frames. For warmth, they used fresh cow manure in a layer about a foot thick underneath the soil to create their "hotbed."

Our great-grandmothers put their plants down in a pit below the ground level with cold frame sashes on top to gather the sunlight. These pits could accommodate very large begonias and ferns and tall plants as well. That is how the parlors in the old Victorian mansions of a hundred years ago were supplied with huge house plants, which they displayed on stands. About the only drawback to the pits lies in their accumulation of water if they are not sealed well at the top.

Cold frames, pits, and cool greenhouses are ideal for propagating plants in winter. Cuttings can be planted in large pots or boxes and covered with plastic and simply left in the frame or greenhouse all winter. Only an occasional monitoring is necessary to make sure they have enough moisture.

thoughts from snowbound charleston

To be snowbound in Charleston is a rare experience for any gardener. Snow looks odd indeed on palmettos and palms and on the steeple of St. Phillips, but it does happen about three times in a century.

The snow cover is kind to all vegetation. When leaves and trunks are covered with the protecting snow, the cold winds do little harm as long as they are not strong enough to break down the limbs. It is the sudden cold spells that sweep in from the northwest without benefit of snow that do the worst damage here in the South. Sometimes the temperature can drop forty degrees in four hours, and this is the real trial for all kinds of plants.

Many, many beautiful plants could be grown in southern gardens but for these sudden freezes. Thomas Jefferson had a great passion to grow olive trees in South Carolina and Georgia. He observed how the poorer Italians seemed to live mostly on the olive crop and thought that the poorer people in the South might do the same. So determined was he to send good olive seeds to South Carolina that he went from Paris on a special trip to Italy—by carriage, of course—to send several barrels of olives to Charleston.

Along the coast of Georgia, several plantation owners tried to grow olive trees. Even General Nathaniel Greene had a hand in this project. The young trees would grow for a few seasons, and some of them pulled through a number of winters, but eventually they succumbed to the sudden cold snaps from the northwest, and the project never was a success.

It is interesting to observe how far north different tender plants can be grown. Poinsettias are difficult in Savannah. They can be grown in the most protected places there, but you have to go farther south to find them in plenty. Most plants with milky juice succumb easily to low temperatures. Oleanders have milky juice, but the old red one seems to make it in Shreveport, which always surprises me. They are common from Norfolk southward, but to find them as far north as Shreveport is thrilling. Corpus Christi and the Norfolk Botanical Garden are the places for oleander enthusiasts. The Norfolk Garden has splendid plantings of them thanks to my friend the late Fred Heutte, the founder of the garden. The Oleander Festival at Corpus Christi is a popular annual summer event.

From time to time, during mild periods, grapefruit has been produced along the Atlantic Coast, but not for long. Orange trees still survive in a few places. There is still one in Charleston. The good news is that the citrus geneticists are at last going to give us hardy orange trees from grandma's old trifoliate orange (*Poncirus trifoliata*). Why have they waited so long!

march

catalogue fever

Spring fever is catalogue fever to the gardener. Even gardeners who never grow a flower indulge their fancies with the glorious colors of zinnias, petunias, and marigolds that appear in the January catalogues.

By trial and error, we here in the South have come to learn which of the annual delights in the catalogues are, and which are not, for our gardens. Godetias, clarkias, and salpiglossis are beautiful and fairly long-lasting in gardens up in Canada, Scotland, and Scandinavia, but they soon burn up down South. Along the coasts, they can be raised from seed in the fall to flower for a few weeks in early spring, but they are hardly worth the space they take. Nevertheless, everybody admires them wherever they are grown.

Those of us who like to make color schemes instead of a kaleidoscope of colors can find almost any combination in today's catalogues. The color range is seemingly endless for zinnias and petunias. When it comes to shades and hues of blue and violet, the selection is limited. There are not too many blue flowers to complement the hot oranges and the bright yellows. Most of our "blue" flowers are really violet, lavender, or purple. I find myself searching for "blues" through all the catalogues and even the English lists. We are still waiting for some geneticist prince charming to come forth in the South and give us heat-loving delphiniums.

South Africa has given us a little heat-loving anchusa that really is blue. This year, I see 'Bluebird' and 'Blue Angel'—two varieties that make "blue" ageratum look almost light violet. All the shades of ageratum are most welcome, however. Larkspur these days is a wonderful improvement on grandma's old deep blue-purple, pleasing as that still is in late spring and early summer. It is now as blue as delphinium.

(Actually, it is an annual delphinium.) We have found that if the seeds are sown early enough our native blue perennial *Salvia farinacea* will begin to bloom by midsummer and increase into the fall.

The greatest fire eater of them all, of course, is portulaca. Why do we see so little of it on the blazing hot banks it would cover with enthusiasm? Zinnias, petunias, nicotiana, marigolds, and dusty millers revel in the hot southern sun. Annual dahlias are fun from seed; no two alike, and they will bloom before frost on nice little plants. The South African daisy flowers dimorphotheca, gazania, and arctotis, we have learned, are not cactuses, but like both good drainage and water, too. Annual burning bush (*Kochia scoparia*) and cockscomb (*Celosia argentea*) can act as little shrubs in the border.

a late spring

A long winter and late spring in the South are apt to bring on a season like springtime in Boston and northern parts of the world: everything blooming at once. Here we usually enjoy a more prolonged blooming season than gardeners do in the North. The early spring flowers come and go long before the late ones, and in between we enjoy a good long midseason, too. This year even the red maples have not bloomed. The woods look like the middle of winter still. Of course, the alders have hung out their tags, however reluctantly. Hazel tags are ready but refused to give off any of their golden pollen when I shook one yesterday. The spicebush (*Benzoin aestivale*) generally flowers on time no matter how long the winter, but the trailing arbutus buds are still tight. It looks as if this winter has frightened everything to death!

All this will end in one glorious burst. Gardeners know what happens when that first hot day suddenly comes upon us. The Chinese magnolias will pop open, the azaleas will light up, the cherries will open—this year probably early and late ones almost together. This is the way spring comes to the Arnold Arboretum in Boston; like the bursting of the famous one-hoss shay—"all at once, nothing first."

Daffodils and all the bulbs with winter foliage like the various kinds of spider lilies need fertilizing right now while their foliage is on and the bulbs are making buds for next year. Actually they should have been fed in the fall, but they respond to a spring feeding to some extent. If you forget, and if they need food, they will skip a year and fail to bloom for you. I now have, for this very reason, a lot of foliage and no bloom on my daffodils in crowded old patches that have been there for years. If they are fed now, even very old stands of the common trumpet daffodils that have not bloomed for a long time will respond and flower a little next year. Then when the bulbs are taken up and divided there will be more of flowering size the first season after you plant them.

Fine shrubs and trees that may be on the starvation margin can be saved for several seasons with a good feeding. It is a shame to let a fine old shrub go down for lack of food.

With all the rains all over the South, the daffodil shows will come off on schedule. Camellia buds were tight in South Georgia and Alabama two weeks ago. This year they can combine daffodils and camellias for some dazzling shows!

hyacinths

The love of hyacinths is very ancient. The name comes from Hyacinthus, beloved of Apollo, who met his death at the hands of Zephyr, the wind. Apollo then said, "Thou shalt be a new flower inscribed with my lamentations!" The Greeks have always made wreaths of the fragrant wild hyacinths for their festivals and for brides-maids. Be all that as it may, it was a lucky day for gardeners in Europe when the Dutch discovered that their rich soil retrieved from the sea would grow the finest hyacinth bulbs in the world. Only in the south of France and a few other places are there any other such hyacinth bulbs produced.

Hyacinth lovers are unabashed at their fondness for these fragrant early flowering bulbs, and so were many Greek and Persian poets! No other flower is so sweet in the last cold days of the year. In the course of their development by the Dutch, they lost a little of their fragrance. The wild hyacinths I imported some years ago from Turkey do have more fragrance than the big, fat, named kinds. Perhaps the strong scent can be reintroduced into the cultivated ones. A single floret from a wild one scents a whole room!

In the eighteenth century there were two thousand named varieties of hyacinths. By 1730, the trade in Dutch hyacinths had become enormous. The English, who had not had many cultivated flowers in their gardens until the Dutch William of Orange came to reign with Queen Mary at Hampton Court in 1689, could not get enough of the new hyacinths. They "learnt" to grow them in glasses and to force them into bloom in the winter.

Old southern gardens have many fine old hyacinths hidden away in them. Our grandmothers liked them and planted them in their gardens, where they grew and multiplied happily in the southern warmth. In addition to the big, named kinds, the Roman and French Roman hyacinths with many smaller and more graceful spikes of blue and white flowers became popular here. They like the temperature of our soil. In fact, the florists of Europe discovered that the Dutch bulbs could be forced into earlier winter bloom if they were first taken to the south of France and grown on for a year.

One of the ardent collectors of the old hyacinths of the South has been that marvelous gardener, Jo Evans. Southern gardeners are in debt to Jo for saving these precious old gems.

some interesting "new" plants

Several particularly beautiful plants that have been in southern nurseries and on plant stands for some years, now have proven their worth in our yards and gardens. Gardeners who are not acquainted with them will be pleasantly surprised when they see them for the first time. Of "new" trees, perhaps the most popular and spectacular is the ornamental pear called 'Bradford'. This early flowering dazzler was selected at the U.S. Department of Agriculture station at Beltsville, Maryland, some forty or fifty years ago out of seedlings of the 'Callery' pear.

It all started back around 1915 when the Oregon Station of the U.S.D.A. brought in some Chinese pears to see if they could breed some trees that could resist the terrible fire blight common to pears. Oregon, of course, is the source of those gorgeous pears we get in our stores in winter. The 'Callery' pear's progeny did help with fire-blight resistance. One of the relatively thornless seedlings of 'Callery' was particularly beautiful with its snowstorm of white, early flowers and foliage that turned all sorts of beautiful colors in the autumn, so it has now been introduced to the public as an ornamental tree. The tiny pears are no bigger than garden peas, but the early spring blossom and the brilliant fall coloring are outstanding.

Some camellia gardens in the South now are growing the white-flowered, winter-blooming shrub called *Abeliophyllum distichum*. This Korean native has been in cultivation in the United States since 1938 in the cold northern sections and is perfectly winter hardy. Here in the warmer South, it flowers right in the winter—sometimes around

Christmas in the coastal areas—and elsewhere with, or even before, the winter jasmine after Christmas. It can be really startling at a time when you are still wearing a heavy overcoat and gloves! Abeliophyllum is very much like forsythia in everything but color of flowers and rate of growth. The white flowers will astound you in the cold weather, but the plants do not run away like forsythia.

While it is not at all plentiful, you can find another white-flowered beauty, loropetalum, in some nurseries. This one is not so early. It flowers along with the forsythias or a little earlier. It is a broadleaf evergreen belonging to the witch-hazel kinship. The tiny white flowers look just like witch-hazel flowers. They are produced so thickly, however, that they hide the small, dull green leaves and are dazzling in effect. Loropetalum can be pruned into an exceedingly handsome hedge or grown simply as a free-standing shrub.

astilbes and the like

Astilbes are moisture-loving perennials with ferny leaves and ethereal spikes of white, pink, or red flowers. Sometimes they are called spireas. They were very popular back in the last century, especially as potted plants brought inside to flower for Easter. For some reason, they have not been seen much in southern gardens for a long time. You can see them in the big public gardens as waterside beauties, but few private gardens seem to have them.

While astilbes like moisture, they do not have to have the side of a pool. They suffer badly from drought but will grow in a perennial border if you do not let them lack for water and if you will water them copiously when the flower buds begin to arise. The fine, ferny foliage of these plants and the delicate spikes of tiny flowers give a light, airy touch to plantings, especially around pools, where they contrast perfectly with the heavy fat leaves and big flowers of water lilies. To heighten this contrast in the flower border, you can plant something with coarse foliage next to them.

The new named varieties I saw in England the summer of 1974 are especially beautiful. These have come into American catalogues of perennials. Wayside Gardens (Hodges, South Carolina 29695) has brought in good astilbes from the Continent all through the years, especially the German varieties. The newer plants vary a great deal in height—from one foot to five. Groups of from three to ten look good together, though a single plant of the taller kinds is a graceful and delightful accent. They seem to go on and on for a long time in flower. After the flowers have gone, the spikes hold color, lengthening the show.

Another fern-leaved plant for water's edge or for drier locations is filipendula, with large, fluffy, white, flattish heads of flowers that look as if they were floating on air. This is a native American from damp meadows. In southern meadows and damp places, goat's-beard (*Aruncus dioicus*) and queen-of-the-meadow (*Filipendula ulmaria*) are two more moisture lovers that can be used around pools. These are spireas in effect (the filipendulas used to be included in the genus *Spiraea*) that will go on blooming through the summer months. They like to be where you drain water off from your swimming pool or lily pool. All the native meadow plants are tough and require no special attention.

break up clay with gypsum

Gardeners do not seem to realize that they can improve the texture of heavy clay soils with gypsum. This can be done without digging or plowing. It takes only a season or so for gypsum to work. You can simply spread agricultural gypsum over your beds or around your shrubs at the rate of approximately 50 lbs. per 1,000 square feet and let the rain wash it into the soil. Agricultural scientists say that the penetration of the gypsum is at the rate of about six inches per year. Since this chemical does not burn or change the soil chemistry very much, it can be applied at any time of the year and on both acid lovers and lime lovers.

It makes clay soils more porous and easier to handle. On very heavy clays, it is recommended that one or two pounds of gypsum be stirred into the bottom of each hole when you are setting out new trees or shrubs. It will eventually provide more porosity in the clay structure and make it easier for roots to grow out as well as penetrate downward.

Underneath some yards and gardens, there is a hard clay floor or subsoil. If you have this under your area, you will have noticed it when you dug holes. In such places, water remains just below the surface or over the hardpan, and tree roots sometimes fail to penetrate the barrier. A few applications of gypsum, six months apart, will often soften up hardpan and definitely improve gardening above it.

Since it is calcium sulfate, it supplies needed calcium to plants and a little sulfur. It is definitely not going to make plants grow because it has no nitrogen, phosphorous, or potassium in it, so your regular fertilizer schedule will need to be maintained.

japanese cherries

When the Japanese flowering cherries (*Prunus serrulata*) began to appear in Europe, the Japanese names got very mixed up. It took the work of several men in England and in the United States to straighten them out, but we gardeners are still confused by the oriental names and by so many beautiful trees with blossoms so much alike.

There are some quite distinctive cherries, however, that are fairly easily recognized, and these are the ones that we are coming to know by name and character. Of course, we all know the weeping cherry, grafted up on top of a standard. This kind has been, perhaps, the most popular of all because of its weeping form. Actually, the weeping cherry is merely a pendulant form of the very early flowering 'Higan'. By now, this breathtaking early mass of light pink has joined the weeping form in southern parks and gardens. There is also an autumn-flowering form of the 'Higan'.

The best-known columnar cherry is the white 'Amanogawa', the name of which translates "Milky Way." These straight little trees allow for the planting of a flowering cherry in very narrow or restricted places. David Fairchild introduced 'Amanogawa' from Japan to the United States in 1906.

Five hundred years ago, the Japanese were growing the double cherry 'Fugenzo'! The flowers are pink, fading to light pink, and flowering at about the same time as the popular 'Kwanzan'. Fugenzo means "Goddess on a White Elephant." This variety is also listed under the names 'James H. Veitch' and 'Kofugen', to add to the confusion!

'Kwanzan' is now possibly the most popular of all the double pink Japanese cherries in America. The bronzy young foliage is beautiful by itself before the flowers appear. The deep pink flowers are two and one-half inches across and have as many as thirty petals. I have always enjoyed the strange color effect that the flowers and greening young leaves produce; they give the impression of light greenish yellow together—a very subtle effect, indeed! Two hundred 'Kwanzans' were planted along the Tidal Basin in Washington with the 'Yoshinos' and are probably responsible for the great popularity of 'Kwanzan'. Most of the Tidal Basin cherries are 'Yoshinos', given to Washington by the Mayor of Tokyo, and planted in 1912.

We in the South have found that Japanese cherries of the kinds we plant are rather short-lived. Perhaps this is partly because of their very heavy flowering habit. My English friend Collingwood Ingram, the pioneer promoter of oriental cherries, told me when I was in London the last time that if Japanese cherries are given some shade, though they will not flower as heavily as in the sun, they will live longer.

south african wild-flower rescue

So passionately do the South Africans love their wonderful wild flowers that they rush out with trucks and landrovers to rescue them when they are threatened with destruction. When a new area is going to be bulldozed for construction, a regular trek is organized to go and fetch the big aloes and splendid shrubs and bulbs back to the towns, botanical gardens, and private gardens. As many as two thousand trucks and vehicles assemble before seven in the morning. The removal of plants is directed by men with loud speakers. The number of plants per individual is fixed, and before night, every wild flower and plant has been removed. This operation is as amazing as the taxi cabs that rushed out to save Paris in World War I.

There are more kinds of wild flowers in South Africa than in the whole of the United States put together; we can hardly conceive of their bounty. Only in Texas do we have miles and miles of perennials and annuals in bloom over unbroken stretches. At the Cape of Good Hope, there was once a cold climate. Many of the flowers there seem to "remember" this cold because they can stand up to the cool parts of the southern states. Some, like the red-hot pokers, can be grown even in our mountains here.

Here in the southern United States, we have begun to make some progress in saving our own wild flowers. Texas began planting them along its roads some years ago, and a regular harvesting program for annuals was worked out. Since they must come from seed each year, the plants are harvested like hay when the seed is ripe. Then the hay is spread over the area where the flowers are wanted next year.

In the states from Virginia to Texas, the public is becoming more and more aware of the destruction of native plants. In North Carolina, we transformed an Advisory Board into the Botanical Garden Foundation, Inc., so it could receive funds and hold lands for botanical purposes. I hope that the fourteen other southern states where I travel, lecture, and study will create similar organizations. Conservancy movements are springing up all through the South, and the state highway systems are getting into the act with planting programs for our native plants.

Of special importance is the matter of saving some special areas where native plants are particularly plentiful. These "habitat tracts," as we botanists call them, should not go into the parks because they will surely be destroyed there. They should be set aside under police protection and visited by small numbers of people at a time. We simply cannot put these areas back if we lose them.

bluebells

The bluebells that we grow in southern gardens are really Spanish, not "English" bluebells, as we like to call them. Actually, these Spanish bulbs are much finer and showier than the real English species common in the woods in the British Isles. Spanish bluebells (*Scilla campanulata*; syn. *Endymion hispanicus*) are some of the very easiest bulbs to grow in part shade underneath trees if the soil there will support them and if they are given a top feeding of bone meal and a complete fertilizer every year to keep them ahead of the game in their competition with tree and shrub roots. They enjoy a depth of three or four inches. Most gardeners know better than to plant bulbs of any kind underneath maples.

If the leaves are left on the beds of bluebells planted under trees, fertilizer in pellet form can be scattered over the leaves right now. While the bulbs are in leaf, they will get the greatest benefit from this food. Do not use plain fertilizer in the ordinary dust form; use pellets that will keep the fertilizer from getting down into the bluebell leaves where it may rot some of the bulbs.

The bulbs are beautiful white, knobby things that look almost like ivory. You would never guess, unless you looked very carefully, that these beautiful white objects are made up of thick scales just like a scale-bulb lily. The scales are fused tightly together and hardly show at all.

The harvest of these bulbs is a really wonderful gardening experience; there will be dozens in each place where you planted only one. Some of them will be round, some long and finger-like, and they are almost snow white and easy to find!

There are no comparable bulbs that come in blues, lavenders, and pinks for the spring landscape. They have been developed into some very subtle shades of blue lavender and even into dusty pink! The pink is a rare color—almost the color of the tube or "cup" of the flower of the "pink" daffodil, 'Mrs. Backhouse'.

Even a few of them, as occasional spots of blue or white or pink, are very beautiful in a garden. The colors are clean. 'Excelsior' is a deep bright blue. 'King of the Blues' is deep sky blue. 'Mount Everest' and 'White Triumphator' are pure whites—the latter the tallest of bluebells. 'Queen of the Blues' is a sort of purplish blue which I think of as being very "French." 'Myosotis' is possibly the nearest to a true blue, and 'Queen of the Pinks' is dusty pink.

You will not be able to resist gathering bluebells for the house because of their wonderful colors and stiff stems. The flower stems are as hard as wood. When you tug at them, the whole stem will suddenly come up, all the way from inside the bulb and give you a real shock. While this does not seem to injure the bulb, it is probably better to use very sharp clippers and clip the stems as far down as possible.

the blue effect

Two of the most reliable, longlasting, and *blue* flowers for southern gardens are the blue *Phlox divaricata* and its form *laphami* and the Spanish bluebells. The perennial phloxes and the bulbous bluebells flower at the same time and create the "blue effect" many gardeners so long for—especially this gardener.

One of the most stunning sights in my arboretum this week is masses of blue phloxes in bloom underneath the greenish yellow flowers of the wild buckeye bushes (*Aesculus sylvatica*). Two years ago, I added some patches of bluebells in shades of light to dark blue—and some of the dusty pink ones. All of these plants are light and airy and full of butterflies attracted by the almost imaginary odor of the phloxes. The greenish yellow candles of the buckeyes seem to float over the tender young foliage, and the ground is carpeted with the blue phloxes and bluebells. Walter Gieseking, the pianist, used to collect butterflies amongst my bluebells.

Our native blue phlox comes in several variations. Some forms have a distinct little notch in each petal. The lapham form has no notch, or very little, and the plants, once you have them established in your woods, will spread unbelievably fast all over the place. The seedlings will come in all shades of blue to pure white, some with a purple eye, some with none. The variations are extremely pleasing. My plants of the lapham type came from northern Louisiana and are very drought resistant. I must have dropped a piece at the top of a hill because they have now spread themselves all the way down—seventy feet—to the bottom. The hillside is a hot, dry, rocky site, but this blue phlox can really take the heat or it never would have taken up residence there. I have noticed how well it does on the hot, dry hills where the Battle of Vicksburg took place long ago.

pruning notes

At long last, it is warm enough to get outside and do some pruning. In the absence of truly dwarf and really slow-growing trees and shrubs, gardeners have to at least touch up their woody plants every season or so. More and more plants that are true genetic dwarfs are coming to America from Japan and Europe. When John Creech started going to Japan to study the ornamental plants in landscapes and gardens some years ago, I knew that we would eventually be receiving more of these handsome things for our gardens. Dr. Creech is the former director of the National Arboretum in Washington, and many of us have enjoyed seeing the bonsai collection there.

The object in reducing the size of shrubs is to retain their characteristic shape and habit while making them smaller. The easiest thing to do is to prune them into balls, but it is not too difficult, once you get the hang of it, to reduce their size and still retain their personality without making cannon balls.

Lots of people are terrified at the thought of pruning their *Magnolia grandiflora*. These evergreen trees and our native cherry laurels (*Prunus caroliniana*) are actually two of the most prunable trees in the world. To reduce them, simply remove the long growths that were made last year. You can go back still farther and shorten the longest branches if the trees are really getting out of their spaces. Do not be afraid to start reducing magnolias and cherry laurels when they are still only ten to fifteen feet tall. (Never remove the leader unless you are making shrubs out of them.) If you wait until the trees are too tall to reach any but the lower limbs, you will have to use ladders to prune them.

The forsythias that dazzle us with their marvelous gold each spring are some of the most rampant shrubs. Wait till they have flowered, and, just as the leaves are beginning to come out, go after them and bring them down to size. Even at Dumbarton Oaks in Washington, D.C., where there is a veritable mountainside of forsythia, they have to do heavy pruning every year or so to manage them. In spaces really too small for them, forsythias can be held down by a good annual pruning.

People are always puzzled about pruning the Kurume and other evergreen azaleas because they grow a new story each year. Try to resist that urge to plant these or any azaleas in spaces that will be too small for them after they are grown. They will continue to try to grow upward and outward, no matter what you do. Of course, the tall new growths can be removed and the new growth more or less forced to take place laterally, but the azaleas will always win! Lighten up on the fertilizer to hold down the big growths.

The long, lusty growths that pyracanthas made last summer will bloom this spring and provide berries this coming fall. If they are just too big for you, and you have no way of training them on something, you can remove about a third of each one. Do it when they are in bloom so that you will not cut off absolutely all of the tiny flowers and thus destroy all the autumn crop of berries. It is a lot of trouble to espalier a pyracantha, but it is extremely handsome when treated this way. A hot, south-facing wall is not too good for this because of summer red spider; east, west, or north is better.

travel notes

The redbuds were just opening when I left Savannah after my lecture there on February 25th. Last weekend, at the end of March, they were just opening, along with the early cherries, in Washington. People were enjoying watching the cherry buds open right before their eyes in the plantings around the Tidal Basin. Many of the old trees planted in 1912 are still there, their venerable trunks leaning over the water and dangling their lovely flowers intimately within reach of loving hands that cannot resist touching them. It really takes a gray day to show off the delicate early cherries—or a misty or foggy night. Night lighting turns them into positive magic.

I also went to the National Arboretum—yes, we do have a national arboretum! It took years to persuade Congress to establish one, but the nation acquired some 400 acres on Bladensburg Road where it joins New York Avenue, and we subsequently added to that a neighboring old brickyard to accommodate the numbers of trees and shrubs a national arboretum should have. The "we" I am using here is you and I, for it is our arboretum. You should go and see it!

Most gardeners have no idea how many gorgeous Chinese magnolias there are in cultivation. A whole hillside of them in bloom at the arboretum was enough to make me gasp. The odor, in spite of a high wind, was delicious. Perhaps the most exciting Chinese magnolias are the pure white ones. Imagine a larger flower, and wider, than the familiar *Magnolia soulangeana*, and imagine a whole tree of these magnificent creations. A few old gardens and cemeteries in the South have ancient specimens of this amazing tree (*M. heptapeta*). The Chinese call it the Yulan or Lily Tree, and it has long been one of their very favorite trees. They have embroidered it on their fine fabrics and pictured it in their art. I have admired these oriental magnolias at Gloster, Mississippi, where Sarah Gladney has her young "magnolia-etum" as I have called it. Down there oriental magnolias are almost winter-blooming trees.

In contrast to the large-flowered pink, cherry pink, and salmony pink magnolias were the smaller-flowered kinds with many narrow petals. These little trees look almost as if their flowers were cut out of paper. They are the ones which we call the lily-flowered magnolia (*M. liliflora*), one of the splendid varieties of which is named 'Water Lily'.

All the early magnolias at Arlington were glorious last weekend. It is seldom that these early flowering trees are not burned by the late frosts here in the South. We are usually grateful if the frosts will spare them to us for three or four nights before turning the flowers brown. But this was the year to enjoy them, and the crowds at Arlington were drinking in their beauty and the scent which swept down upon us as we ascended the hillside through the cemetery.

large shrubs into small trees

Many of our large shrubs can be trained into a small tree shape when they get big enough. In Charleston the other day, I was constantly running into delightful small trees in the little gardens between the houses built so close together. In these enclosed and very limited spaces there were numerous handsome old ligustrums which had been left to grow up and shade the walks and little gardens that are such a pleasing part of that city.

Of course, there were Japanese privet (*Ligustrum japonicum*) trees aplenty, for Charlestonians have long since learned the value of these small evergreen trees, which are actually of Chinese origin. Each one supports one pair of mockingbirds. Robins had come to eat the seeds of the palms, and the resident mockers were raising the devil and trying their best to drive the robins away from the privet berries. Charleston gardens also boast more little trees of what southern nurseries have always called glossy privet (*L. lucidum*) than do those of Savannah or New Orleans. For some reason, the slower-growing glossy privets have been appreciated here and allowed to grow up into small and very handsome specimens with one stem. The trunks have a way of growing this way and that in a sort of zigzag form which is almost oriental.

Since the camellia and azalea crazes brought on the elimination of so many fine shrubs, it is delightful that Charleston gardeners did not dig up these very useful old privets that came into their yards and gardens as great additions to the evergreens in the early part of this century. Today, these little trees actually enhance the beauty of camellias and azaleas by their contrasting foliage and shapes.

Even a common old privet hedge specimen (*L. vulgare*) has been allowed to grow into a tree on one Charleston street. And I was astounded to walk right up to what southern nurserymen call an Amur River privet (*L. amurense*) with a handsome trunk that I could not reach even halfway around with both hands. The cold winter had caused this delightful specimen to lose its leaves. It reached up to the third story of its house and must be a great comfort as a shade tree in the hot Charleston summer.

Most of the large shrubs like the privets and photinias—even the camellias, both *sasanqua* and *japonica,* are delightful and very handsome as small trees. Very often, when large shrubs are planted too close to the house or to a walk, they can be allowed to stay simply by the removal of their lower limbs. They need not always be destroyed or removed. One has to be careful, however, not to expose their trunks suddenly to the hot sun. In very open places, the limbs had best be removed a few each season, until the trunks are fully exposed.

april

september charm

When April comes in the door, it is not as long as you think till September! Now is the time to plant several perennials which will make your late August and September garden a really colorful place. In many southern gardens, this late summer period is drab, with nothing much but liriope and other purplish things. If you plant the Japanese anemones and several of the new anemones that have drought resistance bred into them from the Hupeh anemone, you will have handsome flowers in white and several shades of pink come August and September.

The old white Japanese anemone (*Anemone hupehensis*, var. *japonica* 'Alba') likes a cool spot on the north side of a house or wall. It may burn up in severe summers if it is grown out in the open. It likes light but not a great deal of direct sunlight, and this is the reason why we do not often see it in good form. Nevertheless, there are gardens in Monroe and Shreveport, Louisiana, where it grows in cool places. The newer hybrid anemones can stand more sunlight. They stand up wonderfully to drought, too, and can be counted upon to produce some of the freshest flowers of late summer. To me, they look as if they were made of china.

The old 'Alba' has single white flowers on tall stems, while 'Whirlwind' is double white. 'September Charm' and 'September Sprite' are pink and are two drought-resistant ones that flower in late August here in the South. The earliest of these to flower is the big tall silvery pink (*A. vitifolia* 'Robustissima'). 'Margaret' and 'Profusion' are both big pink varieties to be found in some catalogues.

For hot places such as those on the edges of terraces—especially those covered with paving—the brilliant *Sedum spectabile* is an excellent heat resister. There are several named cultivars of this excellent perennial—in deep rose, pink, and white. Colchicums and liriope look good with these sedums. When these and the yellow sternbergias (*Sternbergia lutea*) come into the seed stores in early July, they can be added to your color scheme.

For a big perennial foliage plant that is beautiful in late summer you might plant bocconia (*Macleaya cordata;* syn. *Bocconia cordata*), the so-called plume poppy. It is up to three feet tall and has gorgeous leaves with silvery undersides. The flowers are borne in a long, white plume and are not showy but add contrast to the big leaves. This old perennial has almost disappeared from gardens—maybe because it tends to spread if you do not control it. There is no more beautiful summer background plant, however, and some gardeners even feature it right on their terraces.

less-known azaleas

Some of the less-known azaleas (azaleas have all been reclassified as rhododendrons) will be of interest to azalea lovers over the South. The Macrantha azaleas, for instance, will prolong the season of bloom in your garden for several weeks after the regular season of Kurumes is over. The Glenn Dales are startling with their amazingly different colors and very large flowers. In recent years, azalea lovers have been trying out the Rothschild Exbury azaleas with their huge yellow and orange and lemon-colored flowers.

The original old Macrantha azalea (*Rhododendron indicum*) that was introduced by southern nurseries is a spreading evergreen plant that does not begin to flower till the Kurumes are finishing. It is a good deep pink, and there is a white form of it, too. This remarkable flowering shrub will get bigger and bigger as the years go on, mostly by spreading out. Some old specimens I know are ten feet wide but only four or five feet tall, so this one should always be used at the front of any planting. In Japan long ago, Macrantha azalea gave rise to a whole race of late-flowering hybrids called Satsuki, the May-flowering favorites of the Japanese today. Our nurseries usually have some of the Satsukis labeled Macrantha or Gumpo. They all have a neat trick of reblooming late in the summer, after they are well established. The hurricane rains seem to encourage them in this flowering after midsummer. In some gardens, they are almost continuous bloomers.

The late B. Y. Morrison, when he was the head of the United States Department of Plant Exploration and Introduction, spent a number of years in an azalea-breeding program at Glenn Dale creating large-flowered azaleas which would be hardy to the low temperatures that the Charleston azaleas could not take. If you are a mountaineer or hill gardener and long for the big-flowered azaleas which you see along the Atlantic and Gulf Coasts, the Glenn Dale azaleas will be safer where temperatures go sometimes to zero. Back in the thirties, I warned the gardeners in Monroe, Louisiana, that the tender Indicas they were planting might not make it through a big freeze. I arrived, several years later, just after such a freeze and found the plants they had brought up from the Gulf Coast killed to the ground or split by the cold. The Glenn Dales were created by Mr. Morrison to prevent just this catastrophe, and the Satsukis will do the same today.

Lord Rothschild's Exbury azaleas have in their blood the most beautiful orange and yellow azaleas in the world, including our flame azalea (*R. calendulaceum*) of the Appalachians. If you grow them, you must make sure that they do not get dry. Plant them in the coolest place available because many of them wilt badly when the sudden heat strikes us in mid to late spring when the plants are in full flower. They will be in bloom in the nurseries, and the gorgeous colors can be selected to your taste.

some wild beauties

The best time to move your tiny blue woods irises is right after they bloom. As soon as the blossoms fade on these small beauties, new roots come out just beneath the tiny fans of leaves, and the rhizomes begin to grow. If you do not have any in your woods, the botanical gardens will tell you which nurseries raise them instead of collecting them from the wild.

Both the little blue *Iris cristata* and the blue and orange *I. verna* will make their new growth quickly and produce flowers for you next year if you will move them at this time. Actually, they can be successfully transplanted at almost any time, but they will rarely flower the next year unless they are moved just after flowering. A little bone meal in the soil works wonders with both species. The delicate foam flower (*Tiarella cordifolia*) and some Christmas ferns (*Polystichum acrosticoides*) or the small ebony spleenwort fern (*Asplenium platyneuron*) make

"The great silvery white meadows of atamasco lilies that used to be such breathtaking sights throughout the South are disappearing."

splendid companions and contrasting foliage with the irises. Then you can add a trillium or so to the group and any other small woodland flowers like wild phlox, alum-root (*Heuchera americana*), crow-poison (*Zigadenus densus*), and fly-poison (*Amianthium muscaetoxicum*). All of these like shady places where the leaves are left over them from year to year. Botanical gardens will tell you how to raise them.

Nature rarely seems to put together some of her showiest flowers, but gardeners like to plant the coral woodbine (*Lonicera sempervirens*) where it can climb up on something and show its color off next to a white fringe tree (*Chionanthus virginicus*). There is no better red and white combination, and these two just improve in size and vigor from year to year.

The great silvery white meadows of atamasco lilies (*Zephyranthes atamasco*) that used to be such breathtaking sights throughout the South are disappearing. Atamascos love meadows with cows grazing over them. The manure from the cows keeps them well fed and being trod upon seems to do them no harm at all. It is very easy to grow your own atamasco lilies from fresh seed gathered in the meadows just after all the lilies have turned red and flowering has ceased. Take the seed heads home, and as soon as they will shatter from their receptacles, shake them out onto a seedbed which can be kept from drying out. Keep the tiny grasslike seedlings moist for a few weeks, and you will have hundreds of tiny bulbs in two months. Seedling atamascos can be left in their seedbed a year or two or may be moved to a permanent position right after they go dormant the first year. They will grow best in moist places, but I have seen them growing perfectly in ordinary gardens. To hurry them on to blooming size, you can water them with weak liquid fertilizer. Of course, liquid cow manure is what they would really like most!

vagaries of april

April is the month when the seasons can jump from winter into summer without benefit of spring here in the South. Newly transplanted trees and shrubs are subjected to hot winds and temperatures soaring near the nineties. Most of us are on the end of a hose trying to keep roots alive while nature is searing the new foliage! The nights are mercifully cool or even cold, but the days. . . .

Soak hoses are a big help underneath new shrubs and trees. Old buckets with a small hole are wonderful. You can set one by a new shrub to leak all through the night while you sleep. Throw a few spoonfuls of liquid fertilizer in the bucket, and your plant will get instant feeding. Mulches are definitely in order in April. They will keep the soil cool around new trees and shrubs while the roots are sending out fresh little feeders and will spare you from the hose long enough for you to get on with the numerous April garden chores.

It is better to feed the whole garden at one time than to do it piecemeal. Inevitably, I forget a patch of bulbs or some starving shrubs unless I make myself do it all at once. Left unfed, a plant has to survive as best it can until the next feeding.

As soon as the leaves of daffodils begin to turn yellow, clumps of the bulbs can be lifted. The big leaves of colchicums will suddenly turn yellow and be gone in a hurry in the southern April heat. At least we do not have to worry about their decaying foliage the way the English do. They are always fussing over dead colchicum leaves. No matter how deeply you plant colchicums, they will come to the top, and you will find the strange-shaped corms right under the surface. Maybe this is why they seem to thrive in gardens; most of our gardens have rich soil on top.

Cold winters lately have frozen lots of gladiola corms. We used to leave them in the ground with impunity, but now is the time to replace any frozen corms with new ones. Do not let them dry out in the spring heat. Here is hoping the winters will not continue so cold or we shall have to dig gladiolas in the fall and store them just like northern gardeners do. Modern "glads" are the product of tender South African species crossed on the more cold-hardy Mediterranean species.

Dahlias have also succumbed to the cold winters in some gardens. So we shall have to order new ones from the dahlia specialists. If you want to raise some dahlias from seed, the catalogues offer seeds of the dwarf varieties. Planted now, they will be up in a jiffy, and the little plants will bloom by the middle to end of August. Prize dahlias can be lifted in the fall without separating the roots and kept in a cool, dry place all winter.

tall bearded irises in the landscape

There are several things about our southern climate and weather that should be taken into consideration when we plant the bearded irises in our gardens and yards.

The late bearded irises happen to come into bloom right with the first really hot spells after our cool spring weather. A hot wind often dries out the flowers. They are fairly good bank holders but if they are planted on some dry, south-facing bank, where gardeners often transplant the excess from their garden, the flowers are apt to be burnt up.

The translucent flowers of bearded irises are disappointing when seen with the sun shining directly on them. Roses are thick petalled and look good with light bouncing off the petals, but irises are most beautiful planted where the light can be seen shining through the flowers from one side or the other. Siberian (*I. sibirica*) and Japanese iris (*I. kaempferi*) are thick petalled like roses, but all of the bearded kinds have thin, translucent standards and falls that glow when light comes through them. By the time they flower, the light here in the South is very intense out of doors. Where they have some dappled shade they are delightful and well worth all the work it takes to grow them. Probably the easiest place for gardeners to locate them in order to get some shadows over them, is where they will get midday sun and some shade in the morning and in the afternoon. Not many people spend much time in gardens in the middle of the day.

They are always delightful planted in clumps here and there because the upright sword-shaped foliage is handsome and contrasts with the leaves of other garden plants. Try planting clumps in different places in your landscape to see how the light behaves at different times of day. In places where they make a telling effect, you can plant larger groups. For massed plantings the irises of one color are the most effective. The multicolored varieties give a rather messy effect and should be reserved for single big clumps.

feed, feed, feed

Now that the leaves have come out, gardeners are assessing the damage from this cold winter [1977]. The large-leaved form of gardenia (*Gardenia jasminoides fortuniana*) was hurt, and even the common, smaller-leaved "Cape jasmines" (*G. jasminoides*), so popular in old cemeteries, were burnt. Many of both were killed back to the ground. It remains to be seen which ones will come out again and which are dead below ground. They will soon let us know.

Yaupons and wax myrtles from the coastal country did not like the extreme cold at all. Many were burnt badly, but the twigs are alive and coming out all right. The foliage has looked terrible for two months.

These two borderline shrubs—on the borderline of hardiness for the Middle and Upper South—responded remarkably to a little protection. There were some yaupons and myrtles—even great big ones—that had enough radiation from buildings to stand up to even the cold winds from the west. In England, the walls of many houses are covered with pyracanthas because these walls provide just enough protection to keep them alive. They survive there out in the open only in the warmest areas.

The greatest casualty of last winter, above the coastal plain, was our beautiful dwarf yaupon. In hedges of it, the sporadic damage to the plants is puzzling. Right in the same hedge, side by side, some plants were killed way back, some were slightly burnt, and some remained in good condition. Why? Very few, if any, of these plants seem to be killed to the ground in most neighborhoods. For a few years, hedges of dwarf yaupon are going to undulate up and down very strangely until we can bring the sizes together!

Now is the time—between now and the middle of July—to feed and nurse back to life our damaged shrubs. Feeding every ten days and some extra watering will bring lusty new growth. The root systems are still there and will respond. Several different feeding methods can be followed. One of the most effective is to punch holes about a foot apart in concentric circles around your shrubs and trees and fill them to within an inch of the top with dry fertilizer. Then water the area heavily with the nozzle off. If you use liquid fertilizer, pour the liquid over the area where the holes have been punched and water heavily.

Most gardeners know that woody plants may not harden off properly to withstand cold weather if they are fertilized much after mid-July. Growth on cold-damaged shrubs and trees may be very erratic. After the end of May, the new growth can be pruned a bit to guide their future shape.

snowballs and other viburnums

Gardeners are sometimes confused with the many kinds of snowballs and other viburnums. All the snowballs are viburnums, but there are a great many other viburnums, mostly with white flowers. The common old snowball (*Viburnum opulus* var. 'Sterile') that our grandmothers grew is still in southern gardens making a beautiful show in spring with its pompons that are first green, then white. This is the common, native snowball of Europe. Its red berries (without viable seeds) are highly prized. In our snowball type, there are no berries because all the flowers have turned into "petals."

Just as the dogwoods begin to play out, the Japanese or Chinese snowballs come onto the scene with double rows of either flat bunches of flowers or snowballs. There are several kinds of these orientals widely grown all over the South. Our own wild black haw (*V. prunifolium*) and blue haw (*V. rufidulum*) open right with the dogwoods. In lowlands here in the South, the nannyberry or sheepberry (*V. lentago*) touches up the landscape with its autumn color. Another viburnum that has pink to red autumn color is the Japanese *V. dilatatum*, a big shrub like the rest, which holds its bunches of dry red berries all winter and into the spring, when the birds finally eat them.

There are three evergreen viburnums: *V. japonicum*, *V. davidii*, and *V. tinus*. The leaves of the huge *japonicum* are thick and shiny and it is one of the really spectacular broadleaf evergreens of southern yards and gardens. We used to think this one was tender, but the cold winters have certainly disproved this theory. Although this grand big shrub has been in southern landscapes and gardens for thirty years or more, people always seem to be astounded by its winter beauty and the size of the big leaves—almost as big as those of *Magnolia grandiflora*.

V. davidii was named for a French monk who discovered many new plants in China. In England, *davidii* is often seen as a tall ground cover, but over here it wants to grow to two or more feet. In winter, it is covered with the most unbelievable blue berries against the evergreen leaves. This beauty is appearing in cans on our plant stands now.

V. tinus is an old favorite in the South and is often called laurustinus. Our grandmothers loved this one for its flat bunches of pink buds and white flowers that open during mild spells in winter. There are now several named varieties of laurustinus—some with attractive reddish tones in the evergreen leaves and with deep red buds and pinkish flowers. Even up in the hills laurustinus will bloom in winter if given a warmish place away from the cold west winds.

In earliest spring, the sweetest of all the viburnums opens its small heads of pungent flowers. Southern gardens now have big specimens of the fragrant *V. carlesii*. A hybrid type of snowball plant that is really spectacular was created in England in this century—*V. carlcephalum* —with *carlesii* as one parent. The specimens I know are now twelve feet tall and still going up. The flowers have all the fragrance of *carlesii*, making this the first fragrant snowball viburnum.

petunias

Petunias are perhaps the easiest of all annuals to grow. A whole bed of these dazzling wonders can be raised, from seed to bloom, in thirty days, and they will grow anywhere in sunshine, except in wet places.

Our modern petunias come in all shades of red and pink to violet and blue. Almost any color scheme you can dream up can be created with combinations of these beauties. The addition of yellow varieties in the past few years makes it possible to put together a really stunning light yellow and "blue" that is a relief from the fiery annuals of summer. A bed of white and blue varieties is positively cooling to look at.

All of the amazing array of petunias in the seed catalogues have come from just two wild species which the Spanish found when they discoverd Mexico and South America. The wild kinds were not very showy, and one would never have believed that such a treasure chest of splendid color was locked up in these two species. It was not until 1831 that the Europeans paid any attention to them.

While we treat petunias as annuals, they are actually perennial. Just before frost, I used to cut a few plants back, pot them up, and bring them to a sunny window in the house. Before Christmas, these plants would recover and begin to flower again. In Florida and even elsewhere in some of the warm winters we used to have here in the South, petunias would survive the winter months. They are apt to bloom themselves to death, however, if you do not keep the seed heads cut as soon as they show up.

One of the easiest ways to raise petunias from seed is to sow them on top of good soil in shallow pots called seed pans. Such fine seeds are easiest to sow if you will mix them with equal amounts of fine sand and scatter the mixture carefully, trying to get it as evenly spread over the surface as possible. Do not cover the seeds with soil. Cover them just barely out of sight with powdered charcoal. The worst enemy of the tiny seedlings is the fungus called "damping off," and the charcoal will prevent this catastrophe. The shallow pans can be watered by setting them in water and allowing it to rise in the soil from below. For some reason, this old method of growing plants from fine seeds has been lost to modern gardeners.

Petunias can be easily propagated from cuttings which root quickly in pure sand or, if you do not wish to be bothered to keep the sand watered every day or so, in perlite and peat or sand and peat.

summer bulbs

In our great passion for daffodils and tulips, we often completely forget that there are some very beautiful summer bulbs for southern gardens. The shapes of bulbous flowers are a relief from all the big, round zinnias and marigolds, and some of the bulbs have the element of surprise that is always a joy in gardens.

Certainly the little zephyranthes are a surprise when they suddenly come from nowhere, overnight, and bloom in a hot summer garden. The name for these little bulbs actually means windflower. Best known to southern gardeners is the South American *Zephyranthes candida* which blooms near the end of the summer and is often called summer crocus by gardeners in the southern states. This little white flower likes us so much that it has spread itself about. In late summer, the abundance of small white flowers is refreshing. The foliage is almost evergreen in warm sections.

Some gardening neighborhoods have a pink zephyranthes that sends up a series of little pink, lily-like flowers, off and on, after rains throughout the summer. You can make this one bloom by watering it heavily after there has been a week or two of dry weather. This one is *Z. grandiflora*. There is another pink one, *Z. rosea*, common in Puerto Rico. Most catalogues advertise the bigger one as *rosea*, but *rosea* is a little flower not much bigger than a nickel. Except along the Atlantic and Gulf Coasts, it must be covered with a winter mulch. Once you see the bright pink flowers in Tallahassee or Mobile or New Orleans, you will be willing to cover it. Mountain women have always loved the different kinds of zephyranthes. You can see pots—sometimes old kitchen pots with holes in them—full of even the little tender ones like *rosea* in bloom on mountain porches in summer. In winter, the little bulbs are taken in to keep them from freezing.

There are two yellow zephyranthes in the catalogues of annuals and summer bulbs. *Z. citrina*, like the intense pink *rosea*, will not live out of doors in the Upper South without a winter cover, but is well worth planting for its small yellow flowers. You can plant a pot of it and take the pot in to dry up when October comes. A larger, butter yellow variety of *citrina* is named 'Ajax'. This is almost surely what you will get when you order what the catalogues call *citrina*. 'Ajax' is a big-flowered hybrid that is hardy out of doors in winter if you will simply throw some leaves over its spot.

Plant all these little bulbs in the border on your terrace. They can even be tucked in between some stones for protection near the front of your intimate planting where you sit in summer. There they will give you many surprises and thrive under a loving eye from year to year.

in praise of phloxes

All the phloxes are wonderful garden plants. From early spring till late summer, some kind of phlox is in bloom in our gardens. Some of them seem to be such delicate little plants that it seems impossible that they would survive the cold winters that freeze the soil an inch or two down where their roots are. Our blue spring phlox (*Phlox divaricata*) can endure what seems impossible droughts in summer as well as deep freezes in winter. It is hard to believe that out of some sixty wild phloxes, all but one species native to America, we grow in our gardens varieties of only a few.

Varieties of *P. subulata*, the moss pink, which became so popular in the early days of the rock-garden craze in this country, brighten walls and old rock-garden sites and have spread themselves by seeds into all sorts of places. The tiny, scale-like foliage is made for drought resistance, and in the hottest, driest places in the sun—even right on rock faces—you can count on this plant to thrive and increase. Today, there are many named varieties in perennials nurseries. Why we do not plant *subulata* right underneath redbud trees puzzles me greatly.

Following right upon the *subulata* varieties and overlapping with them is another wild phlox of the moss-pink type. This one is *P. nivalis*, usually pink, but occasionally white, and it is found in old fields and on the edges of woods in the Atlantic coastal plain and west to Pensacola. In the pines, there is quite enough sun for this plant. Along highways where mowers work over them to cut weeds and grasses, both *subulata* and *nivalis* thrive in spite of the mowing. In fact, the mowing removes their competitors for the sunshine they love, and they are spreading everywhere they get a start all over the South.

Between the moss-pink types and the tall summer phloxes, there are a few medium-height phloxes that come in mid-spring. There never have been many of these, but the white 'Miss Lingard' (*P. maculata*) is a real gem if you can find it in a perennials catalogue or in some old garden. 'Miss Lingard' has always had one weakness, a kind of wilt, but any wilted plant can be quickly dug up and burned, and there is no trouble keeping this phlox in the garden. A lot of very sophisticated catalogues do not offer 'Miss Lingard', but bless Pat Donofrio at Carroll Gardens, Westminster, Maryland 21157—he has preserved it.

Summer phloxes, those masses of color in late summer, are all derived from our two tall, purple, wild meadow species. What you have to remember about them is that, although they come from wet meadowlands, they will grow in gardens if you will only take the nozzle off the hose and flood the plants once a week just as they begin to show buds. This watering will make them bloom and bloom and bloom and bloom—longer than almost any other summer perennial.

the "riot of color"

The "riot of color" advertised in seed and nursery catalogues for over a century now has caught up with us. If you do not believe it, take a good look at the mixture of strong colors in our southern yards and gardens. Joseph's coat was not as garish as this!

It is time that we began to plan color schemes for our properties. A color scheme is ten times more effective and a thousand times more pleasing than the hodgepodge we see everywhere. In the past fifty years, the new flowering cherries, the new crab apples, the new flowering quinces have come into our landscapes. When all these disparate colors are thrown together without plan on the front lawn, the result of all our work is largely lost in the mixture. The subtleties of each shade and hue are swallowed up in the "riot of color." Even if you think you like this, take a look at some planned gardens and see what the planner has achieved.

One front yard I saw this spring had the following riot: 'Kwanzan' flowering cherry with bronzy leaves (just going out), three red crab apples, a row of purple red azaleas, a bank of *Phlox subulata,* plus one big red-flowering dogwood! The mixture was so utterly astonishing that it really constituted a traffic hazard. Nothing seemed to belong to anything else. It was the red dogwood, however, which really added the final insult. The only thing missing was a redbud, but they had stopped blooming by then, thank heaven.

Something white might have helped this awful mixture of colors. White, because it is all colors together, can often alleviate a bad color scheme. There are white redbuds for the earliest color burst. The small *thunbergii* spirea, the upright, old double-flowered *prunifolia* spirea, pearlbush (*Exochorda grandiflora*), and loropetalum are some common early white shrubs. White crab apples, particularly the small Japanese crab (*Malus florabunda*) that has such charming apple-blossom-pink buds that open up white, are especially useful with the other kinds. These small, spreading trees make a nice contrast to the larger, more upright crabs. Dogwoods can nearly always be brought into any color scheme to cool it down.

We do not have too many yellow things in our spring palette. Yellow jessamine (*Gelsemium sempervirens*), kerria, and the delightful, light yellow Banksia rose are in bloom with the cherries and crabs. Earlier, we depend upon forsythia and daffodils. The new golden forsythias are a bit brazen, but the forsythia *spectabilis* is a soft, easy-to-use yellow. This cultivar flowers more profusely than any other forsythia.

flower color

Up until 1941, gardeners and horticulturists had no authoritative way of describing the colors of flowers and foliage. Then the Royal Horticultural Society of England published their *Horticultural Colour Chart*. It was a delightful experience to place flowers on a little piece of black cardboard with an opening that showed rectangles of "colour." You guessed the nearest color to your flower at first and then came closer and closer until you matched your blossom to the chart and discovered its name and number. The textile business had long had names for the colors they used in dyeing, and artists had given names to colors down through the centuries. At last gardeners could ascertain flower and leaf colors in order to describe them accurately.

In 1961, the society brought out color fans based on the chart. Flower-show judges have had color fans which they have used for several decades in this country.

The official names of the colors are fascinating. Some colors have come from flowers or fruits, like Orange, Lemon Yellow, Flax Blue, Ivy Green, Sage Green, Fern Green, Willow Green, China Rose, Plum Purple, Wisteria Blue, Persimmon Orange, Marigold Orange, Poppy Red, Cherry, Buttercup Yellow, Primrose Yellow, Marigold Orange, Poppy Red, Canary Yellow, Mallow Purple, Begonia, Cyclamen Purple, and Fuchsine Pink.

Some color names are very, very old. Lemon Yellow has been in use since 1600, Indian Yellow since 1735, Fire Red since the end of the fourteenth century, Poppy Red over 200 years, Coral Pink since the sixteenth century. More recently, in 1912, Mauvette was given authenticity. The *Colour Chart* lists our native Stokes' aster (*Stokesia laevis*) as an example of this color.

Here are a few of the more interesting colors with their examples given by the chart: Dawn Pink with the example of *Camellia japonica magnoliaflora*. Hurrah! Now we know what color one of our favorite camellias is! Its official number is RHS 523/3. Our little wild gladiolus found around old house places (*Gladiolus byzantinus*), sometimes called Jacob's ladder, is Rhodamine Purple. Garden pinks are mostly Cyclamen Purple while pomegranate flowers are Mandarin Red. The Japanese *Rosa rugosa* that many of us grow is Fuchsine Pink—actually magenta, the color that was so popular a hundred years ago. Would one ever have dreamed that our red dogwood is Empire Rose! Plum Purple seems to fit the old deep purple *Iris kochii* that blooms so early. Finally, there is another camellia described as Carmine. Our dear old camellia 'Chandleri elegans' is the one. This color name is very, very old, having come through several languages to us. It is the color derived by the rug makers of the Middle East from the cochineal bug! You may be dizzy with "colour" after all this!

may

dividing fall perennials

Now is the time to think about the glorious months of September, October, and November in the garden. These months will be full of an abundance of flowers if we prepare for them in May. We in this country never get the most out of fall perennials the way the Europeans do, because we let the clumps stay in the garden for years and years till the soil is spent.

May is the month to dig up those crowded clumps of chrysanthemums and asters of all sorts, prepare the soil, and replant the biggest, healthiest pieces and, if you have room, even the smaller ones.

A big, tight clump of asters or chrysanthemums can be divided by digging around it and turning the clump on its side. If the soil cannot then be shaken off the roots easily, turn the water hose on it, full pressure, and wash away all the soil. It is then a real pleasure to divide the clumps into any size desirable. Dig the soil deep with a nursery spade and incorporate some humus, fertilizer, and bone meal. When the soil is dug deep this way droughts will not bother your plants in hot summer.

If you cannot get to this job in May, it may be done as late as July, but even single stems with roots will grow into handsome clumps by fall if you do it now. When the plants are six or eight inches tall, pinch out the buds and make them branch. Do it again some weeks later and perhaps several times more to keep them at the height you want in the garden.

From September till frost, you can have a big show if you grow some of the following flowers: spider lilies (*Lycoris radiata*), sternbergias (yellow), colchicums, fall crocuses, amarcrinum, the new Japanese anemones, physostegia, the new varieties of *Sedum spectabile*, 'Heavenly-

Blue' morning glories, dahlias, chrysanthemums, asters, Michaelmas daisies (*Aster novae-belgii*), the blue plumbago (*Ceratostigma plumbaginoides*), and the late-flowering annuals like tithonia—to name but a few.

All sorts of color schemes can be made with masses of chrysanthemums and asters. The main thing lacking is blue in our fall gardens, but the old perennial ageratum (*Eupatorium colestinum*) makes wonderful masses of deep lavender, and the annual ageratum, planted fresh in August, will make patches of genuine blue along with the plumbago. If enough "blue" asters are planted, the effect will be pleasing indeed.

If you have a fence available, plant 'Heavenly-Blue' morning glories on it or let them ramp over any available shrubs nearby. They are stunning climbing amongst the orange berries of the old orange or yellow pyracanthas that color up in late August and September before the red ones.

night flowers for the terrace

There are several kinds of night-blooming flowers for the sitting terrace that can be a real evening garden event. A number of plants produce their best fragrance and open their flowers most flagrantly after dark. The largest plants for evening bloom on the terrace are the crinums, the big night-blooming cereus, and evening daylilies, but the smaller nicotiana, petunias, and mignonette are very effective. These all produce wonderful night fragrance, but nobody is there in the dark to smell them. Planted on the sitting terrace, they will charm you with their evening magic.

Crinums are never appreciated in the hot garden during the day since many of them droop in hot sunlight. We do not get up early enough to see them in the morning, and in the evening we leave them to waste their charms out in the dark garden, so they never really get the opportunity to show their dazzling beauty. A clump of crinums on or near enough to the terrace so that a spotlight can be turned on them when they flower can be a great joy to look at after dinner. Even apartment dwellers with only a sitting terrace can create this show. The clumps increase in size, from year to year, and will eventually produce as many as one hundred stalks of bloom. They bloom better if they are not divided. They are ravenous feeders, and you must be sure to keep them fed every ten days during their blooming season to maintain the huge foliage and keep the flowers coming. The most continuously flowering crinum is probably 'Cecil Houdyshel', product of, and named after, that wonder plantsman from California who died some years ago. I got many plants from his nursery. His catalogue had a logo picturing a handshake in front of a big shell. Perhaps no one on the West Coast knew more about bulbs than Cecil. His crinum will flower almost continuously from early summer till frost if it is continuously fed. It will thrive in spite of some shade.

While *Hymenocallis narcissiflora*, the Peruvian daffodil, is not long-lived on the terrace, it is delightful in the evening, and the foliage is not so large as to demand a lot of space. If you search for them, you will find several cultivars of this plant in seed and bulb stores right now. They must be planted at once to keep the flower buds from drying out and will bloom before you get them home if the day is moist!

Mignonette (*Reseda odorata*) is an old-fashioned flower with a scent that was once immensely popular. Moderns either like it or dislike it very much. It, too, is usually wasted out in hot gardens where we seldom go very much in the day. On the terrace in the evening, it provides a compelling fragrance.

The old white nicotiana provides the strongest odor. The modern, colored forms do not seem to come up to it. Even a single plant with as few as three or four of the long, tubular flowers will scent up a whole backyard or garden. Plant a few in pots, and you can move them about, give them away, or take them into the house. They are as tough as their cousins the petunias.

irises

The tall bearded irises seem to have stolen the show to such an extent that one seldom sees any of the other good old tried-and-trues of this genus. Even the showy Japanese irises (*Iris kaempferi*) are seldom seen in gardens these days. The old yellow water flag, *I. pseudacorus*, is so rampant that wherever it has been planted it has fended for itself, but the *spurias* and Siberians (*I. sibirica*) are now seldom seen.

At Dolly Madison's garden at Montpelier, near Orange, Virginia, three weeks ago, I saw the beautiful white form of the low, flat roof iris. This half-shade lover was once very popular. The type has beautiful deep powder blue flowers with black or brown spots and stems usually less than a foot tall. The white form used to be very expensive. At

Montpelier the original plants had multiplied until there were big clumps of the low, pale green foliage all along a path by a wall. The name of this species is *I. tectorum,* and the plants are about three times as big as our little wild *I. cristata.*

Siberian irises are wonderful stream-side plants. They like the same situation that pleases the Japanese irises. The smaller Siberian flowers come before the Japanese and overlap their season nicely. There are several dark blues, some medium blues, and one or two very light, bright, true blue Siberian varieties. The latter are about as attractive as any blue flowers we can grow. With a few whites in the planting, these blue irises are something to dream about.

A group which never seems to have caught on much is the *spurias.* They are very upright, with flowers much the shape of the bulbous Spanish, English, and Dutch irises, but the *spurias* are perennials, not bulbs. They flower with the tall bearded irises on stiff, upright stems, and the flowers come in some unimaginable colors: shades of near brown, light and dark yellow, near whites with pearly tints. They make excellent flowers for corsages and they used to be used by the florists in place of orchids.

Houston, Texas, has long been one of the places where *spurias* thrive. Beginning back in the fifties, Houston gardeners created a fine test garden for these irises. The modern varieties are really unbelievable! They are best moved in early fall when the white roots begin to grow from the tough rootstocks. You can rob a big clump by pulling off some rhizomes from the edge. Dividing the big bunches of roots is best done by shaking off all the soil you can and then washing off the rest with strong water pressure from the hose. Even after that, you will have a terrible struggle to untangle the root mass. *Spurias* like plenty of water, but, like the Siberian and Japanese irises, they will grow in normal garden beds. If they can be watered well before they bloom, the flowers will be normal in size. In Europe and around Algiers, they grow in swampy places. They also grow in the wadies in the desert country. Wadies are the much-prized watering places. That is why one of the handsomest *spuria* iris varieties was named 'Wadi Zem Zem'.

butterfly bushes

Butterfly bushes are hard to find in yards and gardens these days, though they used to be favorite summer flowers. They are, perhaps, one more casualty of the azalea-camellia craze. Nothing attracts butterflies in summer more than these beautiful shrubs. A very cold winter may cut most of the butterfly bushes down to the ground, but they will come back quickly if the roots are not killed. If you lose yours, you can get another right away, since most of the nurseries that handle them can supply them in pots, which allows them to be planted at any time of the year.

The Latin name for this shrub is *Buddleia*. The whole genus was named in honor of of an English botanist, the Rev. Adam Buddle, vicar of Farnbridge, Essex. Another man of the cloth, Père David, a Frenchman, was the actual discoverer of the bushes in China and introduced them, with many other Chinese species, in 1869.

After the bombings in London, butterfly bushes came back by the millions in the rubble and cheered up all of London. Along with fireweed (*Epilobium angustifolium*), they covered over the ruins with their purple spikes. Swarms of butterflies animated the bushes and added an atmosphere of elegance, much to everyone's delight.

Catalogues contain some superb varieties. While it is the darker colors that seem to attract butterflies more than the lighter pinks and whites, all kinds are frequented by these insects. 'Black Knight', 'Empire Blue', 'Fascinating', 'Flaming Violet', and 'Fortune' are the names of splendid cultivars. 'Purple Prince' and 'White Profusion' are two patented kinds that are highly rated. It does seem a bit strange to patent a butterfly bush because the cuttings root so easily.

Any combination of them with the various altheas makes wonderful masses of color in summer landscapes. They come at a time when hot weather has become a bit tiresome, and they like the heat. If you want them to go on and on, just cut off the spikes before they quite finish flowering. They will respond with a second big show in a week or so.

The genus contains many species. We used to grow *B. lindleyana*, an old favorite that made wonderful cut flowers in summer. In England, the summer and early fall gardens and borders are full of many different kinds. One of them, *B. × pikei*, which I saw years ago at Wisley, the Royal Horticultural Society garden, has fuzzy white leaves and superb spikes of bright pink flowers that are extremely fragrant. We simply must get this one for our summer gardens over here. They can be raised very quickly from seed and both Thompson & Morgan of Ipswich, England, (Thompson & Morgan also have an outlet in Farmingdale, New Jersey 07727) and George Park of Greenwood, South Carolina

29647, offer seeds. May is a bit late, but the seedlings might bloom before frost. In any case, they will flower next year.

beyond azaleas for variety

We southern gardeners have been so carried away with the brilliant oriental azaleas that we have planted hardly any other shrubs for the past twenty-five years. When the gaudy masses of azaleas are gone, there are few flowering shrubs in sight.

Here and there, one sees bushes of gransy grey-beard, the fringe tree (*Chionanthus virginicus*), in yards and gardens. Most of these are survivors from the woods there before properties were divided into lots. As the azaleas fade and roses begin to bloom, this, one of our most beautiful white-flowering native shrubs, provides a sort of waterfall of white fringe. It is a big shrub or small tree that blooms at the same time as the coral honeysuckle, providing a red and white combination in the woods. In gardens and yards, the fringe tree with its huge snowy masses makes an excellent contrast to roses on fences and in beds. There is a Chinese fringe tree (*C. retusus*) which I have seen in arboretums and gardens in Europe. It cannot hold a candle to our native species because the fringe is so much shorter.

As the rose season progresses and the fringe tree ceases, another of our big native shrubs takes over. This one is "storax," (*Styrax* in the botany books). Clusters of drooping, white, bell-like flowers hang from the dark branches. In the southern woods, there are two species of styrax: *S. grandifolius*, with beautiful, big, drooping foliage, and *S. americana*, with upright foliage that reveals the little white flowers hanging below.

Both of our styraxes grow in colonies. It is a great experience to run into one of these big colonies in the woods, as I have done many times in the southern states. Old colonies may be as much as thirty to fifty feet across—all the little tree-like bushes connected to the original by roots. In gardens, a single shrub will soon spread into a handsome group—something the gardener will always prize.

Incense and beads were both made from the "storax" of Europe. There was at one time a great commerce in this product. There was also a gummy substance called storax made from the oriental sweet gum tree and valued as a sort of chewing gum. When North America was discovered, Ponce de Leon's "Gentleman of Elvas," who wrote the account of their travels, became very excited about the gum he found exuding from our native sweet-gum tree (*Liquidambar styraciflua*). He praised it and thought it might be a great item of commerce for mother Spain. The Spanish were too interested in gold, however, to pay much attention to native plants.

ginkgo trees

The ginkgo or maidenhair tree (*Ginkgo biloba*) is the only one of several species in its genus that has survived from ancient geological times. Its beautiful foliage resembles the maidenhair fern. In the fall, the light golden leaves are an arresting sight shimmering in the wind.

Ginkgos have been very popular in the eastern United States. The trees are male and female, but the males are preferred because the females drop a sticky fruit that is foul smelling when it falls. Washington, D.C., and Philadelphia are the ginkgo cities preeminent on the east coast. Ginkgos can be found, however, throughout the southern states, usually in cemeteries and on streets.

Alan Mitchell, director of Westonbirt Arboretum, in England, took an informal census of ginkgos when he was over here with the International Dendrological Society. Mitchell has a passion for measuring trees. It is said that he has measured some 34,000 trees and recorded them. He missed my cocktail party in Asheville because I had introduced him to a young forester, and the two of them were out in the forests measuring big trees all night! Mitchell recorded a big ginkgo 111 feet tall at Longwood Gardens in Kennett Square, Pennsylvania, and another 105 feet tall at the Capitol Park in Washington. Some runners-up were a 96-foot specimen at the Barnes Arboretum in Philadelphia and another one, 92 feet, at the Vanderbilt Mansion in Hyde Park, New York. Alan Mitchell's book *A Field Guide to the Trees of Britain and Northern Europe* is one of the most useful guides ever compiled. Most of our native trees are described in it, and the rest are trees that we grow here in the United States. The book is well illustrated with color and black and white and is probably the best book in print for tree identification.

Ginkgo trees are found wild only in the ancient Chinese provinces of Anwhei and Chekiang. They have always been much venerated by the

Buddhists and were apparently carried from China to Korea and then to Japan whence they were introduced to Europe about 1730 and to England twelve years later. Through the years, many types have been selected out from seeds. There are upright types, weeping types, fat types, and skinny types. It is usually the upright ones that have been planted on city streets since they do not interfere with overhead wires.

bulb-digging and cyclamen-planting time

How can the foliage of daffodils, tulips, hyacinths, sternbergias, and spider lilies vanish in nothing flat! It happens every year. A week ago there was foliage on most bulbs, but when I looked for it on the hardy cyclamens today, it was gone—without a yellow leaf in sight.

All of the above bulbs can be dug right away before you forget where they were and go chopping into them in the summer. This is a great danger where bulbs are grown in beds of flowers. It is heartbreaking to chop a fine big bulb in two. When they are dug this early, bulbs will still have live roots on them. These roots will die anyway and are doing nothing to further bloom in the bulbs next year; the flower bud was formed back months ago. Dig bulbs up in clumps, lay them in the shade in a dry place, and forget about them until they dry out. Then the soil may be knocked off and the bulbs allowed to dry out for several weeks, when they will come apart easily. You can do the same with red spider lilies.

The largest bulbs may be replanted in the garden, and the little ones will come along planted in rows in the vegetable garden. For good effect, replant the big bulbs about two inches apart in groups. Of course, this will hasten the time when they must be again divided, but you will have an "immediate effect," as the old catalogues used to say.

Seeds on the hardy cyclamens are ripe now. You will find them in little round capsules about the size of a marble. Unless you want the ants to distribute your seeds, you can pick them right off the corm, curly stems and all, and let them dry out about a week. Then the sticky seeds may be mashed out of the capsules and planted in woodsy soil with some bone meal scattered over it. Just barely cover the seeds and then put a mulch of leaves or pine straw or bark over the patch. The tiny leaves will show up sometime in the fall after cool weather sets in. In three years, each seed will have produced a little corm big enough to flower. Even one single cyclamen corm will soon populate your woods with plants whether you plant the seeds or not. The ants will carry them as much as thirty feet away from the corm.

Now is the best time to order the corms as well as the seeds of cyclamens. If your seedsman has your order, he will send you corms and seeds just as soon as he receives them after this present dormant period.

gardening under mulches

The present hot weather and drought over the South reminds me of former dry, hot summers in the thirties. Only plants that were well mulched pulled through. If, as predicted, we have another dry summer, we had better get our mulches ready. Underneath a good mulch, watering is reduced to a minimum, and only the lustiest of weeds ever make it to the top. It is easy to pull up the ones which do come through because they are rooted in moist soil.

Leaves, pine straw, bark, sawdust, old newspapers, roofing paper (old) and several commercial mulch papers and metals are available. As a rule, it is wise to fertilize plants which are to have a mulch over them. All but the oldest sawdust will steal nitrogen from the soil for the use of microorganisms breaking down the wood particles. Bark may need some nitrogen for a few years, but plants can be fertilized right through the mulch at normal intervals. Leaf mulches are often too dense to let fertilizer through, so rake them aside once a year and scatter the fertilizer on the ground beneath.

Wood and sawdust wash off sloping surfaces in the rains. If some pine straw is mixed with these, they will stay on the surface better. On large areas, the mulch can be sprayed or sprinkled with a tar material used by the highway engineers to hold up seeded banks. Pine needles are nature's best mulch for steep places. The needles will stick on all but the very steepest grade and break up the rain drops when they fall so the bank won't be eaten away in big downpours. Straw is usually available from seed and farm stores in bales, too, and will hold a bank almost as well as pine needles.

There was recently a great hue and cry about using old worn-out carpets as mulches over large areas in the style of "wall-to-wall" carpeting. This sounds like a good idea. One just hopes that no ancient

"Even one single cyclamen corm will soon populate your woods. . . ."

genuine orientals have such a fate unless they are really completely gone. (Even then, they are very useful as pads underneath good carpets.)

There is probably nothing finer or more decorative than bark for mulching flower beds. We used to have to get it from old wood yards or sawmills, and it was a potential source of wood borers, but commercial bark which you buy from nurseries and stores has been steamed and has no live borers. It is perfectly safe for garden use and is one of the good things that has happened for gardening in this country. At last we have come to appreciate and to save and use many valuable products of our forests.

the large perennials

Some of the large perennials and biennials like hollyhocks and peonies can put on just as big a show in the garden or in the landscape as the flowering shrubs and trees. Even a few clumps of hollyhocks can outdo everything in sight for several weeks in mid-spring. Peonies make enormous mounds of color and then keep their handsome foliage till frost.

The big clumps of daylily foliage, making waterfalls of grassy leaves, need the contrasting forms of the other big perennials. The native blue baptisia (*Baptisia australis*) makes round, airy clumps of blue green foliage, and the spikes of blue flowers are stunning against the oranges and yellows of the daylilies. This tough old wild perennial is not often seen in southern gardens in spite of the fact that it is drought resistant and as permanent as a daylily. Old clumps can grow to be three feet across. After the blue flowers are gone, the short black seed pods are beautiful against the blue green foliage. Every summer, I visit some clumps of baptisia at Blowing Rock, North Carolina, that have been there since 1927!

Even a few clumps of red-hot pokers *(Kniphofia)* contrast well with daylily flowers and show them off to advantage. Where you are growing daylilies in partial shade, the different kinds of hostas will provide rounded clumps of broad leaves that eventually spread into masses. Our grandmothers called these August lilies and often planted them in tubs. They would be surprised to see how many different hostas are available from perennials nurseries today.

In late summer, the big perennial sunflowers of many kinds come into bloom. Some of these natives, like the Jerusalem artichoke (*Helianthus tuberosus*), grow with no care at all in the edges of shrubbery or in otherwise neglected places. Brown-eyed and black-eyed Susans (*Rudbeckia hirta*) are not exactly big perennials, but they make big masses in the summer landscape when they are left alone.

Joe-Pye weed, of the genus *Eupatorium*, and ironweed (*Vernonia flaccidifolia*) are two late-summer and early fall wild flowers that we can grow with no trouble at all along with the perennial asters in the fall. Ironweed contrasts well with the masses of perennial asters and towers above them. Both of these "weeds" are just as handsome as anything in cultivation, and they are right on your ditch banks and in meadows nearby, no matter where you live—even if you are a city dweller.

the rugosa roses

Driving along the highway last week in North Carolina, I almost ran off the road when suddenly, on my left, a huge mass of pink purple attracted my attention. I knew in a moment that it had to be a rose. But what rose on earth could be that color—even more violet than most purple pink roses?

Having gone a safe distance and turned around, I backtracked, getting more and more excited with every yard, till at last I stood in front of a mass of roses six feet high and twelve feet across. Gorgeous rough foliage told me at once that this was a rugosa (*rugosa* means rough) and the color said it must be the celebrated 'Roserie de L'Hay', which the French rosarian, Gravereaux, introduced in 1901 and named for the great rose garden near Paris. Perhaps my nurseryman uncle, John van Lindley, had sold it to the owners.

This marvelous old rugosa is but one of several hybrids that one can buy from old-rose specialists today. The rugosas are all big roses that will provide masses of completely disease-free bushes with dark green, rough foliage for the borders of properties or for backgrounds. They have spreading habits not usually wanted in small gardens but very desirable for large places, where the bushes will provide flowers from spring till frost and then crops of big, red hips in early winter. Rugosas are very hardy to cold and have been most popular in colder climates than ours.

Some of the most famous rugosas are 'Belle Poitevine', 'Blanc Double de Coubert', 'Delicata', 'Frau Dagmar Hastrup', 'Hansa', 'Scabrosa', 'Souvenir de Christophe Cochet', 'Souvenir de Philemon Cochet', 'Mrs. George Bruant', 'Lady Curzon', 'New Century', 'George Will', 'F. J. Grootendorst' (one of the most popular), 'Fimbriata', 'Dr. Eckener', 'Conrad Ferdinand Meyer', 'Carmen', 'Calocarpa', and 'Agnes'.

If you are interested in old roses, you will want to get your bookstore to order for you Graham Thomas's *The Old Shrub Roses* and his *Shrub Roses of Today*. In this country, the best guide to old roses is probably the illustrated catalogue of Tillotson's Roses, Brown's Valley Road, Watsonville, California 95076. This catalogue costs $1.00 and is really an education in itself.

lavender

Gardeners often complain that they cannot keep old-fashioned lavender in their gardens for very long before it dies out. Usually, two things are involved in growing it successfully. The first one is calcium in the soil, since it is not an acid lover. The second is that, even under the best growing conditions, lavender can be short-lived and must be replenished periodically.

It will grow in even poor soil if it can have perfect drainage, lots of sunshine, and calcium. Except in the limestone areas, most garden soils in the South are apt to lack calcium. It is for this reason that delphiniums (heat also gets them), clematis, and lupins do not do too well in our untreated soils. It is easy to add the needed calcium, but gardeners often do not think of it. Scatter about 2 lbs. of agricultural lime per 100 square feet over the surface, or work it into newly prepared beds. Since lime takes effect very slowly, most people apply it in the fall, but it does no harm to apply it at any time. Just do not put it on with any other fertilizer at the same time. Wait a week in between.

Even in England where lavender has been grown for centuries and where the soil in most places is all but too limey, gardeners are accustomed to replenishing their lavender plants quite often from either cuttings or seeds. Nurseries always have a good stock of small plants, and both gardeners and nurserymen raise the better kinds from cuttings in summer. They usually pull off little pieces, taking a bit of the main stem with them, which they call a heel. These will root readily and supply healthy young plants to replace the straggly old ones.

After the winter has done its worst to lavender bushes, they will benefit from a light trimming in the spring, and if you collect the flowers for drying and storing, gather them just as soon as they are open and leave them, spread over papers, to dry in the shade.

Many of the common herbs are from limestone country in southern Europe and around the Mediterranean. Thyme, lavender, rosemary, and many salvias grow along with the boxwood on some of the most impossible looking limestone rocks in the southwest of France. On a trip down there some time ago, I was amazed at the terrific heat, drought, and limey soil where they all seemed to be perfectly happy. Our wet winters—not the cold at all—are hard on many herbs, too. They like it high and dry!

northern virginia gardens

Boxwood is the feature in the gardens of the famous Virginia patriots. Most of the flower gardens no longer exist, perhaps because of the difficulty of maintaining them these days. I missed flower gardens terribly at these old mansions on a recent trip through northern Virginia during Garden Week. I used to visit these gardens with Violet Walker when I was at Woodberry Forest Preparatory School. Violet let me plant things in her garden, once the site of the garden of Dolly Madison.

The garden at Jefferson's Monticello seemed terribly neglected and flowerless. Most of the original big trees were gone. Only the old catalpas seemed to have weathered the storms that must rage over this high place where Jefferson planted so many trees and shrubs and flowers. In his *Garden Book*, he recorded innumerable new plants which he was trying out at Monticello. The catalpa, he says, was introduced from North Carolina. Gardeners of today can share his excitement about plants and flowers and the "new" trees in this, the most interesting garden book ever written in America. I am happy to say that the gardens and grounds at Monticello are at last being faithfully restored by a team of historian, horticulturist, and archaeologist. The resident horticulurist is Peter Hatch, one of my favorite students from Sandhills Community College's Landscape Gardening School of Southern Pines, North Carolina. This school is modeled on the Royal Horticultural Society's school at Wisley Gardens, and is supplying America with excellent landscape gardeners.

The builders of the fine houses in Virginia probably never intended for their boxwood edgings to grow up. They were carefully trimmed so the pattern of the bed could be enjoyed like an outdoor rug. Today, many of these borders have been allowed to grow up and block out even the view of the countryside! In England, some of the formal gardens lost their form when the owners went wild over rhododendrons, which today are being removed in some places.

We gardeners who live in the hotter parts of the South will some day have access to *Buxus balearica*, a species which likes hot weather better than the English and even the "American" box. ("American" box is not American at all but simply the big natural bush type of the wild boxwood of Europe and England. English box is a dwarf form of European box.) I first saw *B. balearica* at the Cambridge Botanical Garden. The boxwood garden at the National Cathedral in Washington is always a joy to see, as is the one at Dumbarton Oaks. On a visit there a month ago I found them taking the protective winter covers off the bushes. They cannot afford to let the ice and snow mash and break down such handsome old plants.

june

wild flowers of june and july

While June gardens are full of the masses of gaudy roses and daylilies we love so much, a more subtle show is going on in southern woods and fields. Millions of tiny white umbrellas make up the big white parasols of Queen Anne's lace, in bloom now for nearly a month. Blackberries are ripening in fence corners. Trumpet vines hang out their brassy instruments in a shower from old trees and fences, and several wild flowers in a lower key are blooming in the edges of woods and fields.

Green-and-gold (*Chrysogonum virginianum*) is still in bloom in the woods. The small, orange coreopsis is gone, but one of our longest-flowering wild flowers is putting on a show with its airy blossoms. This one is *Coreopsis major.* The bright golden blossoms seem to float over the plants around them. If you look very hard, you will see that there really are nearly invisible wiry stems supporting the flowers above rosettes of narrow leaves. The stems seem to grow right through their own leaves. Where patches of it are growing with other plants, you will have to strain to see anything but the flowers themselves.

This little coreopsis has been telling me for years how important it is in the summer landscape. I am willing now to give it a high rating for length of bloom and the ability to grow almost anywhere. It will grow, too, in competition with more robust wild flowers. So you may hope that it will take up its abode in your garden or woods. Seeds are ripening right now and will produce a batch of seedlings. Once you have it, it will multiply by the little rhizomes. In the woods, it makes patches of plants—all hooked together underground.

Another of our fascinating wild flowers is called wild quinine in some books, but I cannot find any record of its having been used as medicine. The plant is *Parthenium integrifolium.* Its heads of white flowers look like small asters with no petals, and you can see them along almost any roadside now. The root is a big tuber, and this must have been the source of "quinine." The driest, poorest soil seems to be what it likes.

Also in the driest places the little white-topped or silky asters (*Aster paternus*) are in bloom right now. How they can live in the dry places they inhabit is hard to see. They make neat, small plants that never fail to bloom no matter how high the temperature goes. Perhaps the hairy stems and leaves hold in what moisture there is.

I am always amazed at the number of American wild flowers in the famous perennial border at Hampton Court, up the Thames from London. The border was some six or eight feet wide when I first saw it in 1927. Today, it is fourteen feet deep and should inspire us to cultivate our own wild flowers.

summer

When the temperature goes into the nineties and the orange butterfly weed opens, can there any doubt that summer has come? Butterfly weed (*Asclepias tuberosa*) is far from a weed. It is the most spectacular orange flower in the South's box of summer wonders. Along the highways, it opens the season with its brilliant orange. For weeks and weeks, it makes huge splashes of color, big enough to see even if you are going seventy. That is what it takes in this high speed age; something bright in huge patches. It is one of the very best of perennials for roadside planting for a number of reasons. Its root is deep, deep in the ground and is not likely to be disturbed or pulled up by the mowing machines. If its top is cut off, it has the strength to produce another one immediately, and the second one will flower before too many weeks are out. Even if the top is repeatedly cut off, the plants will most likely still survive.

We hardly need any more orange or yellow to plant with the daylilies, but butterfly weed makes a wonderful companion to these perennials because it is a complete contrast in shape. Furthermore, after the daylilies are long gone, the butterfly weed will still be going strong as contrasting blue flowers come on.

It is easy to raise this perennial from seed. Watch for seed production and get them before they blow away in the wind. Sometimes you can find a light yellow one—a real prize, indeed. Plant them at once where they can remain for one or two seasons. If you fertilize the small plants in the seedbed, they will be ready to transplant next spring. The huge roots of the old plants are difficult to move because of their great bulk and brittleness and because they go to China!

The English have long admired butterfly weed. It was grown at Hampton Court in the perennial beds in 1690! English botanists were fascinated by the leaves both opposite and alternate and at the way the stems will grow in an upright position or lying almost flat. This habit often helps it slip under the highway mowers, keeping its blossom intact.

If you watch a clump of the orange flowers of this plant, you will soon see from its visitors why it got the name butterfly weed. Moths seem to like it, too, and get stuck to the flowers sometimes. Pleurisy or Ache-in-the-Side Plant were the names for it in olden times. Like many plants, it was supposed to be good medicine for a number of things.

plant for the autumn garden

Now is the time to plant annuals and biennials: annuals for the autumn garden and biennials for next year. In the long days and warm soil of June and July, they will germinate immediately and produce a crop of wonderful little plants. You will be surprised at how fast they will grow into big ones during the long days. Of course, you can wait until August to plant biennials, but the ones planted now will produce husky, big specimens that will delight you in next year's garden.

All of the annuals, from marigolds to zinnias, will grow quickly and begin to bloom in late August and early September. Annuals planted in late spring will not have the strength and determination to flower that these later seedlings have. Be sure that your seedlings do not get a setback along the way. Drought is the most likely enemy of midsummer seedlings, so water sprinklers should be handy. During very dry times, use a soak hose and spray seedlings for a moment every day or so with a fine spray to discourage red spider mites.

As soon as they are big enough, the new seedlings can be set out in empty spots in the garden. It is easier to handle them when they are small because big plants wilt badly in the summer heat. Give each a little private fertilizer and watch the magic.

Biennials like foxgloves and hollyhocks are always welcome in the spring and early summer garden. Many gardeners do not realize that both of these favorites may play out and that some seedlings should be raised for replacement, either from volunteers or deliberately sown seed. Usually there are enough self-sown seedlings to keep them going. Catalogues have some very beautiful hollyhocks and foxgloves that you may not have seen. Even if you prefer single hollyhocks, a few of the double ones will emphasize the beauty of the singles. There are also frilled ones and annual kinds that will bloom before frost.

The different strains of foxgloves will surprise you. Some are six feet tall. Some have a strange big flower on top of the spike. There is also a very beautiful strawberry pink foxglove (*Digitalis × mentorensis*) that I raised from seed when it came out some years ago. It is perennial, but it did not stay with me but three or four years. The two- to three-foot plants had very beautiful foliage at the bottom that remained after the spikes dried up.

The old perennial called *Anchusa italica* dies out so easily after a few years that it may as well be treated as a biennial and planted every year or so. It has fuzzy leaves, like those of hollyhocks and foxgloves, that allow it to go through our hot weather. Planted now, it will bloom with the tulips next spring and lend its blue flowers to the color scheme. In fact, it produces the largest masses of blue to be had at tulip time, except for the Chinese forget-me-nots.

holly-feeding time

The green berries on Chinese hollies at this time of the year are as beautiful as any flowers. All Chinese hollies flower earlier than our American species. Their berries are mature when other kinds are still very tiny.

Watch your Chinese hollies for starvation. They are apt to overproduce their berries and use up their food. After a big crop of the gorgeous berries has been produced—and delighted us from October till January—the leaves are apt to turn yellow and even fall off in January and February. The plants are not sick; they are simply starved. If we are going to have fine, big hedges and specimens of these hollies all over the South in public places and in yards and gardens, we must feed them regularly. Feed once or twice between February and the first of July with 8-8-8 or any complete fertilizer. If they are in very poor soil a stronger fertilizer than 8-8-8 may be needed.

Although there are many wild hollies from China, what we call

Chinese holly is *Ilex cornuta*. 'D'Or' (yellow berries), 'Hume', 'Jungle Gardens', 'Lehigh Valley', 'National', 'Rotunda', 'Shangri-La', and 'Shiu-ying' are some of the older varieties. Each year there seems to be a new Chinese cultivar introduced from somewhere because Chinese holly produces so many berries that numerous variations are bound to come about. Incidentally, hollies can produce berries that carry seeds which have no embryos.

The hybrid American holly (*I.* × *attenuata* 'East Palatka') introduced by the late Dr. H. Harold Hume, is another holly which bears fantastic crops of berries in some years. Usually, it wears itself out when this happens, and the trees rest a season or so before they do it again. If this heavy-fruited holly is not fed regularly, it may starve itself to death or go backward for years.

summer-flowering shrubs

Far too few summer-flowering shrubs are grown here in the South. After the great spring show, there are relatively few shrubs to carry on.

One of the most beautiful flowering shrubs in the world is native to the Lower South, the white-flowering buckeye (*Aesculus parviflora*). Yet very, very few southerners have ever seen it. I had not seen it until I ran into it in the Royal Botanical Gardens at Kew in my youth. It does not flower until the early part of the summer, usually after the middle of the daylily season. From the large mass of buckeye foliage, long, spindly green candles arise and take their own good time to develop. In this stage, one would never guess what is going to happen, but all of a sudden, the green spindles begin to fatten. Then, very quickly, they open into candles of white fuzz like so many big bottle brushes.

The white buckeye is not a small shrub when it is grown. It will spread itself over a very large area if allowed to do so, but it can be held down easily by judicious pruning, which it does not dislike. For a dazzling white, there is nothing to compare with it among flowering shrubs. Even the English, who have so many shrubs from all over the world, place it high on the list. One of the largest areas covered with this buckeye can be seen at Longwood Gardens in Kennett Square, Pennsylvania.

Blue, pink, and white hydrangeas are fine summer shrubs because they will grow in sun or shade and provide a wonderful contrast to the daylilies. It is really surprising that so few of them are grown. In Europe these old favorites come in many varieties and are called hortensias and lace caps.

The popular big *Abelia grandiflora* is a splendid summer shrub when it is not butchered or sheared. Its tendency to put up tall new growth seems to irritate some gardeners, who expect it to stay down no higher than three or four feet. When allowed to get its natural height of six to eight feet, it is a beautiful thing, covered with flowers in early summer. We like it here in the South because it has interesting, nearly evergreen leaves with reddish tints and myriads of pink white flowers, which give a white effect. It is not evergreen in the North. You will like it even more if you see it as a hedge around public parks where they have left it to grow to its natural size. If it is not sheared down, it will continue to flower longer than any other shrub during the hot weather and even into the fall.

Smaller in every way except for the flowers is abelia 'Edward Gouchet', which will please you with its neatness, smaller size than *grandiflora*, and its striking purplish flowers. There is another small-leafed abelia with tiny white flowers, usually listed as "U.S.D.A. hybrid."

philadelphia arboretums and gardens

Gardeners who visit Philadelphia may wish to visit some of the country's oldest collections of trees and shrubs. I spent a week there seeing very old trees and historic arboretums and gardens. Media is a convenient center from which to visit most of the arboretums.

Michael James and I went first to see Leonie Bell, whose illustrations for *The Fragrant Year*, by Leonie and Helen Van Pelt Wilson, so charmed gardeners. Leonie showed us her collection of old roses, and then she took us to the Tyler Arboretum nearby. The many ancient, unusual trees at Tyler were planted by two bachelor Quakers, Minchall and Jacob Painter, on land that had been in their family for seven generations. They planted, between 1845 and 1875, more than 1,000 species which they got from Kew Gardens and from John Evans and the second Humphrey Marshall. Today, there remain more than 100 species at Tyler.

The Morris Arboretum at the University of Pennsylvania is a vast collection of trees and shrubs. It is a great education to see such an array of species from all over the world. This arboretum was started in 1932 with a bequest from Lydia T. Morris. It is open from 9:00 AM to

8:00 PM in summer. One should start out with the map in order not to get lost!

The 250-acre campus of Swarthmore College is a joy. Gorgeous big Atlas cedars and unusual conifers will thrill you as you stroll up and down the hill. Swarthmore is the home of the Arthur Hoyt Scott Horticultural Foundation, whose object is to display the best ornamental plants for eastern Pennsylvania.

The public usually thinks of the Barnes Foundation as a collection of art, but the four acres around the Barnes mansion have a tight collection of the best of trees and shrubs. Mrs. Barnes taught a handful of students until she was up in her nineties, and these thoroughly instructed—and fortunate—students are horticultural leaders in many places. Dr. John Fogg took us around. He was very excited about the flowering for the first time of the pink form of our southern yellow-wood tree (*Cladrastis lutea*). We each held the flowers for the other to photograph the delicate pink blossoms. It is absolutely necessary to get permission to visit the Barnes Foundation before going there, but this can be done the day before by telephone.

The famous garden of John and William Bartram, who planted the first botanic garden in America, is in a factory area and is difficult to reach, but it is very rewarding to go there and see how these two Quakers, father and son, who discovered many of our rarest southern plants and grew them and sent them to Europe, operated at home. The little seed house where they dried their seeds is fascinating, and is exceedingly evocative of the simple ways of living which suited our Quaker ancestors. John Bartram, botanist to the King, sent more plants to England than any other collector. He and his son William walked all through both the North and the South and described and collected plants in the areas still occupied by the Indians.

If you visit Independence Hall, be sure to see Leonie Bell's charming garden of old-fashioned roses. The Pennsylvania Horticulture Society's headquarters are nearby. There you will be welcomed, informed of their activities, and shown many of the wonders of their library.

some good old roses still with us

In spite of black spot, mildew, aphids, and neglect, some of the old roses that were popular back as long ago as the Victorian period are still holding on in southern gardens.

Until the introduction of the China rose, gardeners did not expect flowers from their bushes but once a year—in the spring—with an occasional odd bloom in the autumn. In 1837, however, the French nurseryman Laffay introduced a rose that would bloom several times from spring till fall. This was truly sensational, and he then brought forth several more of what came to be called hybrid perpetuals.

Between 1837 and 1890, a whole stream of hybrid perpetuals came into gardens: 'General Jacqueminot', 'Frau Karl Drushki', 'Ulrich Brunner', 'Paul Neyron' followed Laffay's original varieties in rapid succession. American gardens got these almost immediately, and our great-grandmothers planted them here in the South. Since that time, many "slips" have been taken, and thus these good old roses have been brought down to southern gardens of today.

The way to make climbing roses bloom profusely is to wind and bend the stems around trellises or some kind of frame. Rose lovers who have visited English gardens have not failed to notice that lovers of old roses have trained the old hybrid perpetuals like 'Ulrich Brunner' and 'Frau Karl Drushki' on frames and trellises and made them bloom lustily several times in a season. Victoria Sackville-West did this at Sissinghurst most successfully. I am not sure whether Graham Thomas taught her this trick or not; they shared a great enthusiasm for old roses.

Besides the hybrid perpetuals, there are numerous other old roses here in the South. One is the Empress Josephine's 'Souvenir de la Malmaison', an old Bourbon rose. Rose lovers still enjoy the flat, biscuit-shaped, light pink flowers with the fragrance so popular in years gone by. Before the Civil War the old teas were always popular in the South. Old cemeteries like Bonaventure at Savannah and run-down gardens at the old plantation mansions are where we are finding them. The fascinating cemetery at Natchez yielded cuttings to make new bushes for the tea rose garden we are making at Carolina Dormon's house, Briarwood, near Saline, Louisiana.

There used to be hundreds of tea roses grown in the south of France for the perfume trade. I went searching around Nice for old teas at the famous wholesale flower market there in 1954. I walked down the aisles between rows of cut flowers stacked all the way to the ceiling; they were waiting to be shipped to Lyons and Paris. Alas, the old tea roses have disappeared from all but a few catalogues. Our old southern gardens and cemeteries will have to provide them.

The little "sweetheart" rose so well known in the South is really 'Cecile Brunner' if you want to look it up in a book. The bushes get to be fifteen feet tall here. The other day, I saw a huge specimen of the climbing "sweetheart" so big that half of it had had to be removed to keep it from pulling down its arbor!

'Mme Plantier', 'Caroline Testout', 'Crimson Glory', and 'Crimson Rambler' are all still to be found in older or more permanent southern gardens. These old standbys have certainly proven their worth—in spite of black spot, aphids, and mildew!

the old hybrid teas

The 1931 catalogue of Bobbink & Atkins, famous rose nursery of Rutherford, New Jersey, is a treasure of the great roses of that day. Tea roses, hybrid teas, hybrid perpetuals, and many other kinds are listed with excellent color plates. Once more, the question: where are these magnificent roses today? Once more, the answer: in old gardens and yards all over the South. Famous roses like 'La France', which was the first hybrid tea, can still be found because of their good constitutions. The thirties was a period when the hybrid teas held sway as the "re-blooming roses." Long buds and stems and fragrance were what they had to offer.

It is rather surprising that we can still find quite a number of these old favorites: 'Angele Pernet', the "brownish orange rose" of 1924; 'Antoine Rivoire' (1895), the "mildew resistant rose"; 'Columbia' (1917), bright pink that was popular as a florist's flower; 'Dame Edith Helen' (1926) with 60 petals; and the magnificent 'Etoile de Hollande' (1919).

'Etoile de Hollande' is surely one of the greatest roses ever produced. It refuses to give up to pests and diseases. The robust bushes just put out new growth and outgrow whatever attacks them! It is because of their tea blood that these magnificent old standbys survive and go on in the South. The catalogues of the thirties said that flower production would wane in the hot weather but pick up again in the fall. Like their tea ancestors, that is just what they do.

When 'Radiance' came out in 1908, it was hailed as the "easiest grown and most reliable" pink hybrid tea rose over most of the United States. It was not until 1916 that 'Red Radiance' came out and received its great welcome. The South is still full of these two roses. You can get cuttings from old cemeteries almost anywhere.

The hybrid teas with yellowish or copper tints are very subject to black spot, but some of them still survive today. 'Mme Butterfly', 'Rev.

P. Page-Roberts', 'Los Angeles' (salmon pink), 'Mrs. Aaron Ward', and 'Wilhelm Kordes' can still be found. The fragrance of all of these old hybrid teas makes them ever delightful and worth growing.

Old roses of all kinds are becoming more and more popular. A few years ago the Heritage Rose Society was formed by a group of us in the Upper South. Several people are making plans to establish collections of the old standbys. If you are interested in the old roses, you can join the society for $3.00 a year. Subscriptions are handled by Dr. Charles G. Jeremias, Department of Chemistry, Newberry College, Newberry, South Carolina 29108.

flowering trees

Flowering trees provide the biggest splashes of color in our landscapes. Dogwoods and redbuds are the glory of our spring. When they are gone, there are other trees that will carry on with masses of color. We need to become aware of them and use them.

When the lavender cascades of wisteria are beginning to fade, the upright candelabra of the Chinese princess tree (*Paulownia tomentosa*) light up roadsides over the South. Nobody ever seems to plant these trees in yards or gardens; they just come up by themselves wherever there is a break in the woods or a crack in the asphalt in a city. We simply take them for granted and seem to ignore them in our plantings. In other parts of the world, the princess tree is considered one of the most beautiful of all flowering trees. Lavender is not a common color in the landscape. In the colder parts of England where the princess tree is not hardy enough to bloom, the English cut the trunks back to near the ground every year and enjoy the huge leaves as garden features. The princess for whom this tree was named was Anna Paulowna, Princess of the Netherlands (1795–1865).

It is surprising that we plant so few of our native catalpa trees. The tall species that comes from west of the Alleghenies (*Catalpa speciosa*) and our eastern species (*C. bignonioides*), from which we like to collect big worms (the larva of the catalpa sphinx moth) for fishing, used to be great favorites for parks and cemeteries as well as home grounds back in the last century. Since catalpas are not very long-lived, we should begin planting them again. Their fresh tubular flowers come into bloom amidst big, lush, green foliage like that of the princess tree. Although these two trees look alike, they belong to different plant families. When the western catalpa was discovered in the Ohio Valley, there was great excitement about this tall tree. It was found to have wood that is very resistant to rot, so it was grown to supply fence posts and timbers that were to be in contact with the ground. Long after the forest that formed Reelfoot Lake had caved in, decayed, and disappeared, the catalpas were still standing in the water. Perhaps the largest planting of these tall handsome trees is in a big park in southeast Columbus, Ohio.

Just as the flowers of catalpas are fading, the mimosas begin to take over. Of course, the mimosa wilt discourages us from planting these trees. The Department of Agriculture is still trying to find wilt-proof mimosas in addition to the two that are on the market. One virtue of these trees lies in the fact that they can be transplanted in the winter—even big ones—with no soil, but they must be supported well during the first year afterwards.

How can gardeners resist the little goldenrain tree (*Koelreuteria paniculata*)? Right now, it is showing off its masses of golden flowers as an echo of the masses of daylilies everywhere. Goldenrain is easy to grow and flowers when quite small, so you do not have to wait a long time for it. It is small enough to be fitted in almost anywhere and can be trimmed down a bit every year if it gets too big. It is our only golden-flowering tree after the little laburnums. You may have to look for it in cemeteries, old gardens, and parks, but you can grow it easily from seed ripe at summers end, or get it from a nursery.

mulleins

The big fuzzy mulleins that grow along roadsides and in dry places are world tramps; botanists are just not sure where they started out. Most probably they come from the Mediterranean area because there are so many other species all around "the Med." Back in the days before the advent of modern cosmetics, old people used to tell me, young ladies, just as their beaux were about to arrive, used to rub the fuzzy and prickly leaves over their faces to give them color! (All mulleins do not have fuzzy leaves, however.)

The spikes of our native *Verbascum blattaria* have yellow or white flowers that arise from extremely ornamental rosettes of long, crinkled, green leaves. Even if these plants never flowered, the leaf rosettes would be worth cultivating for their appealing symmetry. You can grow this species easily from seed. Watch for the bottom seed capsules to mature, and scatter the fine seeds almost anywhere. When the hundreds of little seedlings appear, either let them grow where they are after thinning or transplant a few to the garden. One of Caroline Dormon's most beautiful black and white portraits is of this plant in her *Flowers Native to the Deep South* (p. 119). She calls it Moth Mullein and notes that it, too, is not really native.

In the Old World, the long taper-like spikes of *V. thapsus* were used for torches, and the plant, much like our common fuzzy roadside species, was called Aaron's Rod, Hag Taper, and Torch. English gardens today have a number of these handsome wooly mulleins. They grow them in perennial borders for their silvery spikes and rosettes. Public gardens like Queen Mary's Rose Garden in Hyde Park in London invariably have mulleins planted with other silvery or grey things like artemisias and silvery annuals. They seem to like them with almost any summer flowers.

In our southern gardens here at home, mulleins like the heat and drought. Since their Mediterranean clime is dry, however, we need to locate them where they will have plenty of air circulating around them. The foliage of the fuzzy kinds will rot if other perennials are allowed to smother them in the long wet periods. The most likely place for them is on a dry hillside. They look well with yuccas, or on the very, very dry slopes where the prickly pear cactus will grow. Mulleins and other plants which make round clumps of leaves are most effective as singles or in groups of three to five, but not too close together.

In gardens, the grey rosettes of the fuzzy species will delight you, summer and winter, as occasional plants in hot, dry places where nothing else seems to grow. The green-leaved kinds can be good accents in groups in the perennial border or as a tall background.

hollyhocks

Nothing in any garden, anywhere, is more exciting than tall hollyhocks reaching for the sky. Hollyhock flowers take the garden's color and lift it right up into space. The effect is both dazzling and airy, and hollyhock colors run the whole gamut from white to red and even include maroon and yellow. They have been the beloved of gardeners since time immemorial. The Chinese, the Venetians, and the Egyptians have grown them in their gardens and developed special kinds to their liking. Since 1573, the English have grown and loved them, and they have spread themselves from seed in American gardens to hedgerows and orchards.

There are few perennials or biennials from which gardeners can have so much for the small effort it takes to grow them. A handful of seeds will produce a hundred plants. Fresh seeds planted as soon as they are ripe will come up almost 100 percent. In fact, the only mistake one can make is to plant the seeds too thickly. Scatter them loosely so that the little plants will have plenty of air and light about them. They are fuzzy, drought-resistant plants, and they grow off rather fast and need room to expand without running into each other.

Modern hollyhocks are even more brilliant than the old ones. There are wonderful colors among them. Some of the double-flowered types have flowers so crowded on the stems that little if any foliage appears at all, making each a solid spire of color. These are interesting, but some of the looser ones are needed to show them off. Catalogues offer us annual or biennial hollyhocks. The annuals will bloom the first year from seed if you plant them in the spring. It is a little late for these in June, but some of the plants might bloom by frost. The rest would be especially big, fine plants for next year. June is a good month in which to sow the seeds of all kinds. In 1971, one of the All America Selections was 'Silver Puffs', a dwarf with loose, semi-double light pink flowers. The Royal Horticultural Society put its stamp of approval on 'Newport Pink' because of its even, clean pink color. Look at the seed catalogues for the various kinds and forms. Even if your doubles revert to singles from seed in the garden, they will be charming. Many gardeners like the old singles best, anyway.

They are subject to rust, so be sure to keep the old, dead leaves pulled off down underneath the big plants. They need air and light and good soil and will mostly take care of themselves. It has been found that they do not get rust in and around industrial towns where there is sulphur dioxide in the polluted air!

dividing tall german irises

New iris fans often ask me how to divide mature iris clumps that have ceased to bloom. When irises do not produce their normal crop of bloom, they may be starving from overcrowding. It is time to relieve this situation by separating and replanting them. If they are allowed to go on multiplying over the tops of themselves, iris rot and borers will likely take over and destroy the whole bed. When you dig them, divide the rhizomes into Y-shaped pieces with two main fans of leaves. This will give you two pieces of rhizome (root) attached to one older one. I usually throw away the old rhizomes. In the case of very fine varieties, however, you may replant some of the old rhizomes that have small fans of leaves trying to develop. It is best to plant these old pieces by themselves and to watch them because they tend to rot. As soon as the leaves have developed, you can cut away the old rhizome.

Tall bearded irises like good drainage. They like lime, too, and bone meal. While they will usually grow in our ordinary garden soil, a sprinkling of agricultural lime over their bed will help them, and bone meal mixed into their soil will give splendid results. Perennials like irises that multiply rapidly always do present a challenge to the gardener. How can we make them bloom the greatest number of years before they must be separated? Faced with this problem in a large collection of irises back when they were just beginning their popularity, I developed a method of planting that would put off the dividing day as long as possible. The whole collection was planted on raised beds for drainage with enough room to walk between the beds. The area was limed, and bone meal was stirred into the soil. Planted this way, it was some six or eight years before they had to be divided.

Single clumps in perennial borders or free-standing at the edge of shrubbery can make a big splash in your garden picture. Dig the soil up and mix in a little lime and enough bone meal to hide the dirt. Then bring in a bushel basketful of good soil and dump it right on top of the prepared area. Pat the new soil down to hold together and place rocks or bricks around it to keep it from running away when frost heaves it in winter. In setting out your irises on one of these humps, use three or four double-fanned divisions. Face some of the fans to grow inward and some to grow outward. This will give good distribution and allow for the clump to grow in all directions.

The humps-for-clumps, we might call them, can be raised right in the perennial bed with the other flowers. The elevation will keep down iris rot and raise the plants just slightly above the other flowers and make them very prominent in both foliage and flower. You can count on six or seven years before division is necessary, except for very rapid dividers.

july

wild-flower seeds

Most of the spring wild flowers in our gardens and woods have now ripened their seeds. Gather all you can find and plant them right now because fresh seeds will come up in a week and give you a fine crop of new plants which you can transplant and give away.

Look for the dried-up tops of fire pink (*Silene virginica*). This brilliant red flower is one of the showiest and justifiably one of the most popular of all our wild flowers in all parts of the South. It grows in sun and part shade in the woods and will amaze you with its response to a spot in your garden, where it will show off even in shady places. It is accustomed to our droughts and has covered itself with some sticky glue to hold its moisture in when necessary.

In wet places, there are seeds of numerous kinds of wild irises getting ripe now. Get the big capsules before they dry up and split. The seedlings will look like grass. A little fertilizer will make them grow so fast that many will flower in two years.

Bloodroot (*Sanguinaria canadensis*) and mayapple (*Podophyllum peltatum*) have ripened their seeds now. So have the pink and the white hartmannias—sometimes called pink evening primroses. It is probably too late to find the little oblong seed heads of trout lilies (*Erythronium americanum*), which should be collected in April. If bluestar (*Amsonia tabernaemontana*) grows in the garden of anyone you know, by all means get seeds and plant them. You cannot even buy this big cloud of blue mist from plant nurseries!

The early flowering moss pinks (*Phlox subulata*) are so easy to grow from little pieces that it is not necessary to bother with seeds. Any tiny bit will grow—even in dry places if it can just be kept moist long enough to make a few roots.

Watch the plants of your favorite wild flowers and collect and plant the seeds just as soon as they are ripe. Our wild flowers are disappearing so fast that it behooves us to multiply them as quickly as possible.

This is that magic time to plant the seeds of perennials and biennials of the cultivated kinds, too. Look in the catalogues and seed stores for Chinese forget-me-not, foxglove, Canterbury bells, the old perennial *Anchusa italica*, pinks, and any other biennials and perennials to your liking and sow them right now. These are the longest days of the year that bring seedlings along in a hurry.

daylilies

The glorious modern daylilies are the most important and showy perennial we have from late spring into midsummer throughout the United States. The shows begin in Valdosta, Georgia, in June, and the season marches northward about one hundred miles every week, reaching Boston toward the middle of July. I recall vividly all the excitement about these flowers when Dr. Stout at the New York Botanical Garden collected all the Chinese hemerocallis species and began crossing them. The most popular nurseryman back in the twenties was that charming and delightful man Bertrand Farr at Wyomissing, Pennsylvania. The subtitle of his catalogue was *Better Plants by Farr.*

Bertrand Farr had the best of everything at Wyomissing. He pioneered most of the good things from all over the world. He bred daylilies, he bred the first "red" iris, he offered the first Chinese tree peonies. When customers wanted something rare and special, his staff would have to get him to locate it in his huge nursery because it was a jungle of rare plants that only he knew at sight. He was called upon as the judge supreme, from Boston to Washington, for the big flower shows. Bertrand Farr and Ernest H. "Chinese" Wilson were two of the most inspirational plantsmen in this century. Wilson spent many years in China collecting plants for the English as well as for the Arnold Arboretum in Boston. His many books describe his travels in China, where he got on well with the people whom he greatly admired and loved. If you like adventure books, you will enjoy his *China, Mother of Gardens; Aristocrats of the Garden; More Aristocrats of the Garden;* and *If I Were to Make A Garden,* which contain much of the fascinating story of plant collecting in China.

With all the new varieties of daylilies, along with the good old ones, we gardeners are in the same position as we were with the tall bearded irises some twenty years ago: we have so many that we do not know what to do with them. People grow daylilies in a jumble with no color scheme at all. These wonderful plants make a big show in the land-scape, and can create unbelievable effects with carefully planned color schemes. For masses of pure color, use the "self-colored" (flowers of one color) instead of the muddy or mixed colors, which do not have an effect at a distance. The light, pure yellows carry farthest. By all means, separate the light lavenders and "blues" from the yellows and oranges. The violets together will astound you. People viewing from a distance will not believe they are daylilies. White shrubs and flowers are good with them. If you can plant the powder blue vitex shrub behind them, you will have a splendid "French" effect, which will be heightened by a few very light yellows.

Red-hot pokers (*Kniphofia*), those long, poker-shaped perennials, provide a contrast in shape to the daylilies. There are large and small pokers, these days, and they come in several colors, including white. Clumps of them will point up daylily beds, and they too are enhanced by the blue of the vitex, which will get bigger and bigger and finally become a handsome, small bushy tree. You can, if you like, cut it back to the ground each year as they do in the North, or as winter often does, and it will come back and bloom like a big perennial.

With such a palette of colors, you can actually make a rainbow of daylilies—from the violets all the way through the reds and pinks to yellows and oranges and white. To do this, pick individual flowers and lay them out on the ground in daylight to create the sequence you want. What a feast of color!

beach plants

Everyone who visits our southern beaches from Maryland to Mexico in the summer is fascinated by the beach plants growing in the sands. It is hard to believe that beautiful flowers, shrubs, and grasses can flourish in the deep sands and withstand the winds without wilting in the hot sun. Most of our cultivated plants cannot take it, but some native plants thrive in this adversity.

Yaupon (*Ilex vomitoria*), the handsome, boxwood-like native ever-green holly, stands right up to the salt spray. Yaupon is, therefore, the best native shrub for hedges and screens at the beach. The evergreen elaegnuses, though not natives, can also take the salt spray and provide variety where much yaupon is planted. The silvery or bronze coating on the underside of the elaeagnus leaf shimmers when the sea breeze strikes it. Elaeagnus, as every gardener knows, makes long new growths. One can take advantage of these growths by training them over an arbor, which will provide a fine, shaded place to get out of the sun and still enjoy the breeze.

Everyone loves the sea oats (*Uniola paniculata*) and the brilliant gaillardias, native to Texas. Another native Texan that has gone up the beach from the South is the Mexican poppy (*Argemone mexicana*), and still another is the roadside verbena (*Verbena rigida*). Of course, the yuccas are always beautiful whether in bloom or not. They defy the salt spray and the sea gales. Showiest of all are the many varieties and colors of oleander. From Norfolk on down to Mexico, they are the real showpieces of summer beaches. Don't miss the annual oleander show if you are near Corpus Christi.

Over the dunes, one finds large patches of green plants, along with the sea oats, holding the sand together. One is the sea elder (*Iva imbricata*), a low shrub. Another is the gray, shrubby croton, and still another is the thistle-like saltwort (*Batis maritima*). (Incidentally, the word *wort* simply means plant.) Then there is the sea kale (*Crambe maritima*), with fleshy leaves filled with water. Back of the dunes on the North Carolina coast, you can find the salt grass or short spartina (*Spartina patens*), and on most southern beaches, the yellow-flowered evening primrose (*Oenothera biennis*) and one of the ground-cherries (*Physalis viscosa*).

Most annuals will flower very quickly at the beaches. Petunias will go through the winters in protected places because they really are Mexican perennials. They are prepared for wind and drought with the sticky stuff they have in their sap. Nicotiana, the flowering tobacco, is a close relative of the petunia and tobacco and has the same equipment. For real brilliance and resistance to salt spray—also for its ability to bloom very quickly from seed—portulaca cannot be beaten. Buy the seeds of separate colors and the double forms for a real show.

an old-fashioned garden

The old-fashioned garden lies on a back street. Tall buildings surround it now. The house sits way back from the street, and the front yard has always had a garden on both sides of the big front walk.

Hollyhocks, blue salvia, larkspur, love-in-a-mist, and lemon lilies—all from the past—crowd each other and all but close up the walk these days. 'Safrano' is in full bloom now along with other old tea roses and old hybrid perpetuals like 'Paul Neyron'. All through the summer, the old teas will be in bloom. 'Duchesse de Brabant', 'William Allen Richardson', 'Isabella Sprunt', 'Devoniensis', 'Catherine Mermet', and 'Sombreuil' will cover their big bushes with fragrant flowers. When autumn comes, these old teas will really "try themselves," as the old folks say.

In the shady parts of the garden, blue and pink hydrangeas enjoy the cool. Clumps of August lilies, or hostas, and red spider lilies will brighten the place in September. Two big crape myrtles out in the sun will soon be in flower. They will carry on with pink when the blue vitex has gone. Large clumps of white crinums have started to bloom now. They will be followed by 'Cecil Houdyshel', the deep pink variety that flowers several times when the old lady waters it from her bucket of cow manure "tea," hidden around the corner near the rain barrel. She has the wine red crinum called 'Ellen Bosanquet' that I gave her years ago. The bulbs have made huge clumps that produce dozens of heads of wine red flowers and stop the traffic on the street in August.

Of course, the little white clematis that now runs over the top of shrubs in this old place will bring on its snow white mantle when September comes. The old lady has never especially liked purple liriope. Her beds are full of perennial ageratum, though. She just pulls it up where she does not want it.

As you would expect, there is summer phlox everywhere—both the named varieties and the purple seedlings that come up in the beds. The habit of giving away "a start" of pretty phloxes, plus the big barrel of "tea," is probably what keeps the big clumps from going backwards. Cow manure comes from the farm every month.

The old roses have not been crowded out of this garden by modern azaleas; neither have the spireas. Over the porch, there is a huge white climbing rose, a favorite of all old-rose lovers: 'Aimee Vibert', introduced in 1828, and the only white perpetual-flowering climbing rose. Not far away is 'Madame Hardy', the old white bush rose with the attractive green eye.

Right now, the old lady is busy cutting back her chrysanthemums and rooting the cuttings. She says the cuttings will be very apt to outdo the old clumps—with a little "tea," of course.

hardy cyclamens

Southern gardeners traveling in Switzerland in summer have wondered whether we could grow the little bunches of *Alpenveilchen* that children sell, here and there, in the European mountains. After experimenting with these little violet-like, perennial cyclamens, we know that, given certain conditions, we can grow most of the different kinds.

The first flowers of *Cyclamen hederifolium* (*C. neapolitanum* in many catalogues) begin to appear through the mulch of oak leaves in my woods before the end of July. This cyclamen is the easiest one to grow if you do not make the mistake of planting it upside down! The corms are available from George W. Park (Greenwood, South Carolina 29647) and other seedsmen here in the South as well as from northern firms.

When you receive your corms, they will look like little flat biscuits. It takes a careful examination to see that there are some tiny, dried-up buds on one side and, usually, nothing at all on the other. Believe it or not, the flat, slick side goes down and the tiny buds go up. The roots of this cyclamen, unlike all the other species, come mostly out of the sides of the biscuit-like corms and grow into the leaf mold and soil mixture which should surround them. *Hederifolium* is different from all the other species. It likes to grow just underneath the surface, in one or two inches of half soil and half humus with some bone meal over the surface. The flat corms should sit on a well-drained base. Coarse sand and soil make a good foundation for them. Since this species of cyclamen lives more than a hundred years where conditions are right for it, no amount of trouble is too much. Drainage will prevent the corms from rotting. A hillside or a raised bed is a good place for this valuable plant.

I brought home seeds from a corm of *hederifolium* over ninety years old back in 1954. The corms from these seeds are today six and eight inches across. They produce more than a hundred little violet-like flowers each year between mid-June and mid-November when the beautiful ivy-like leaves come on for the winter. Nothing succeeds like success. Once you have established cyclamens in a woodland setting, they will multiply from seeds.

All the other kinds of cyclamen can be planted just the way you plant daffodil bulbs. They should be in good soil and about an inch deep.

Planting too deep will prevent the delicate stems from getting to the top. Any cyclamens you can find are worth trying; they are all wonderful, and the season goes from early winter till mid-spring. They are members of the primrose family and are really corm-bearing perennials. Sometimes they are listed under perennials and sometimes under bulbs. Partly shaded locations are good for them, and the winter foliage makes a beautiful ground cover.

july, month of the morning-glory

In the Japanese Floral Calendar, July is the month of the morning-glory (*asagao*, or "morning face"). The flowers that greet the morning with their breathtaking beauty fade quickly with the oncoming hot sun of a midsummer day. Thus, they symbolize to the Japanese, as they did to the ancient Chinese, the shortness of life.

For several centuries, they have been a subject of great admiration in Japan. Japanese horticulturists took the ordinary wild Chinese species and developed it into huge flowers in all kinds of fantastic shapes, from a dragon's mustache to a huge bell. When they became fashionable amongst the wealthy Japanese in the eighteenth century, horticulturists, nurserymen, and gardeners vied with each other in showing their new varieties in the gardens around the fashionable Yedo residences.

At the close of the eighteenth century, there was a sudden cold spell that killed the morning-glories and destroyed the seed crop. The cult was not taken up again until about the time of Admiral Perry's arrival, in the Tempo period of 1830. Then nobles, priests, and princes began paying exorbitant prices again for one seed, and rival horticulturists had their prize plants sent considerable distances by coolie to be entered in the asagao shows of the time.

If you have never seen the huge flowers of the famous Japanese morning-glories (*Convulvulus japonicus*), you can easily raise some of the plants next year from the seeds offered in American seed catalogues. They used to be very popular, but I have missed them lately from southern terraces. They can be grown as single plants in pots or climbing up on trellises or on a fence, or most often, on the house. These delightful flowers are not for those who sleep late in the day. The Japanese used to get up at four-thirty or five to see the asagao open. They had asagao-viewing parties at these hours. One sage commented

"How these little stems can push up through thick oak leaves is a miracle. . . ."—Cyclamen hederifolium

that it was not necessary to serve any refreshment but a cup of tea at such early hours, and thus it was not an expensive kind of party.

Even if you have only some wild American morning-glories, you can enjoy watching them suddenly unfurl their buds at breakfast. Pick the buds the night before and put them in a vase in the dark. As soon as breakfast is on the table, bring out the vase. You will have to watch carefully because the miracle will happen in a split second!

midsummer flowers

Midsummer, and where have all the flowers gone that we used to see in yards and gardens at this time of year! Perhaps the azalea craze, the camellia craze, the daylily craze, and now the rhododendron craze have stolen some of our efforts and some of the space we used to give to perennials.

Back along country roads, the beautiful summer flowers still abound. There are summer phloxes in great masses that have got out of hand. The lavender and purple and red horsemints (*Monarda*) are still there along streamsides. In their native meadows, phloxes and horsemints out-multiply almost any competitors—even the wild sunflowers (*Helianthus*). Perhaps we gardeners are getting too lazy to divide and replant the spreading perennials, but they certainly do provide a lot of color for three or four years before they become overcrowded.

The lavender spikes of the obedience plant (*Physostegia virginiana*), still bloom in the meadows that have not been drained and paved-over for shopping centers. In gardens, the white physostegia has bloomed and gone now, but there are several strong varieties such as 'Summer Glow', 'Rosy Spire', and the very late-blooming 'Vivid' that keep the season going right into cold weather. These tough old perennials will provide a big show every year if they have half a chance anywhere.

The summer coneflowers (*Rudbeckia*) stand up to the heat and drought because they are equipped with a rough outside that resists drying and holds in the moisture, apparent if you feel the rough stems. There are several coneflowers in purple, light and dark yellow, and deep gold. All of the named cultivars are selections from our wild ones.

I miss the grey and silvery masses of artemisia from gardens, these days. The several old-fashioned kinds that grew in grandmother's garden seem to have disappeared. They were called old-man's-beard, dusty miller, and such names. Occasionally, I see some wonderful clumps of the most beautiful of them all, 'Silver King' (*Artemisia albula*), that used to be so popular in late summer and as dried flowers in winter.

The little red *Salvia greigii* from Texas has about disappeared. It was a hot-weather bloomer like the blue *S. farinacea*. 'Blue Bedder', a variety of *S. farinacea*, has become very popular since southerners have finally caught onto this native perennial that stays with us in hot weather. This, combined with the low blue plumbago and the annual torenias, can keep blue going until the veronicas take over in mid-summer. Gardeners seem still to love ageratum and grow it every year. A fresh batch of plants can be sown every month to keep blue going till frost.

It is not long now till the "magic lilies" (*Lycoris squamigera*) will emerge from the ground. If it is very dry where they are growing, and if watering is not forbidden, soak the ground over them and bring the magic, long, green, leafless stalks up overnight.

monardas

Nothing makes a bigger splash of color in midsummer than the various species and varieties of horsemint. These native mints are some of our most pleasant plants to crush and smell. They are also some of the very easiest perennials to grow in gardens or in rough places. In fields and along streams, they color the landscape for several weeks during the summer. The wild bergamot (*Monarda fistulosa*) comes in many shades of lavender to white, while Oswego tea or bee balm or fragrant balm (*M. didyma*) runs the whole gamut of colors from deep violet to white, including the popular red one. In the woods and fields where these plants grow wild, a gardener can pick up many beautiful shades and bring them home. Since the plants are shallow rooted and will transplant easily, they will always live, and, since the South is full of horsemints, there is little danger of depleting them.

In the garden monardas overlap with the daylily season. Masses of lavender monarda are especially fine in contrast to the mid-season to late daylilies. When crape myrtles begin to flower, a real show can be created by planting large masses of monardas where the two will be seen together. Big plantings can easily be maintained for several years by scattering some complete fertilizer over the beds once a year, in the spring. Since the plants thatch together in a tight mass, nothing else has a chance amongst them. In Europe, where American perennials are greatly appreciated, catalogues list any number of monardas. 'Cambridge Scarlet' is one of the oldest selections. Some other kinds listed are 'Rosea', 'Rubra', 'Salmonea', 'Violacea Superba', 'Sunset', 'Perfield Crimson', and 'Perfield Glory'. We can find these same natural variations in our meadows and fields by looking for them if we wish. The color range is unbelievable.

Monardas were named for the Spanish physician Nicolas Monardes of Seville who wrote a series of reports from 1565 to 1571 on the plants of the New World. A collection of these reports was translated into English by John Frampton, a London merchant, as *Joyful Newes out of the Newe founde World*. Monardes described the tobacco plant in great detail. His account greatly excited Europe, where the interest in plants was at fever pitch. Any possible new medicine was of the greatest importance. The accounts of the medicines and food plants of the Indians stirred the Europeans almost as much as did the lust for gold. In the end, the plants were more important.

wisteria

On a visit to Dumbarton Oaks in Washington, D.C., I found no fewer than seven gardeners busy cutting back the long annual growths on the wisteria around the beautiful ornamental pool. The man-hours spent on this project every year must be considerable. When, as a consultant, I first looked over Cypress Gardens near Charleston, I was told that the garden was paying a thousand dollars every year to have the wisteria seedlings pulled up! We decided to eliminate most of the vines and spray the fading flowers of the remaining ones with a chemical to prevent seeding. All this is the reason for my saying, "I get hysteria over wisteria."

The wisterias are gorgeous vines from China, which, like the honeysuckle, have "found a home here." Beautiful as they are, their invasive ways have to be curbed. In summer, they run over everything for ten to twenty feet in every direction. In winter, they pop their seed pods and scatter them the same distance away.

Now is the time to prune them back. Cut all the laterals back to three leaves from last year's growth. If this is done right away, you may stop the lengthening and force the vines to begin the production of flower buds at each node. When the main vines have reached as far as you want them to go, cut them off too. Standard wisterias grown in shrub form have to be pruned almost constantly during the growing season. Even after they have reached maturity, the annual growths come on constantly. The United States Department of Agriculture has learned how to make azaleas grow small and should try their art on wisteria. It would be a real challenge.

The Chinese wisteria (*Wisteria sinensis*) is a beautiful vine that blooms after the popular Japanese kind (*W. floribunda*). Chinese wisteria blooms off and on all through the summer after its initial season. For this reason, it is good to have one of the Chinese vines intertwined with the Japanese to carry on the flowering season. While the Chinese flowers do not come in long chains, their bluer color is very welcome in summer. There is also an excellent white form. If you run into a white one, you can easily root cuttings of it in sand at almost any time of the year. Our little-known native *W. frutescens* (sometimes listed under the genus *Kraunia*) is a delicate vine that will add interest to your arbor. The flowers are in small bunches and of an appealing purplish color.

four distinguished southerners

Four very distinguished southerners were honored by having plants named for them. One of these illustrious gentlemen was an officer in the Revolution, one was a Scottish doctor, one was a diplomat, and one was an early botanist.

I searched all through the cemetery at St. Michael's in Charleston several years ago for the grave of Major Charles Cotesworth Pinckney and his famous wife, Eliza Lucas Pinckney. Charles Cotesworth and his brother, General Thomas Pinckney, were patriots from the start of the American Revolution. Eliza Lucas was the clever young woman who learned the secrets of indigo production. Certainly the Pinckneys deserved a visit to their graves, and I found them right up against the back of the church. One of the treasures of my library is one of Charles Cotesworth's botany books with his own marginal notes, made while he was in Europe. Honoring the Pinckneys is the genus *Pinckneya*, and the only species in this genus is *pubens*, one of the most beautiful of all our native southern shrubs or small trees. Since this showy small tree will grow north of its native range, which starts just south of Charleston and moves southward in the coastal plain, it is really surprising that few gardens have it. While in the air force back in the forties, I found a white form of pinckneya near Bainbridge, Georgia.

The famous Scottish doctor Alexander Garden knew the Pinckneys. In fact, he was their physician. From Charleston, he sent hundreds of specimens of the plants of the New World back to England. Like many Scotsmen and Englishmen at the time of the Revolution, Dr. Garden had to choose between the mother country and the new country. He chose the crown and returned to London when the Revolution started, while his son chose to stay with the patriots. As a result of his great interest in plants, Dr. Garden was made a member of the illustrious Royal Society, and the gardenia was named for him.

One of the really rare shrubs of the South is *Elliottia racemosa*, a plant so choosey that it is found in only a very few places. Since it resists cultivation, one rarely sees it, even in botanical gardens. So it gave me great pleasure when I had the opportunity to show the old specimen at Biltmore House near Asheville, North Carolina, to the International Dendrological Society. The southerner for whom elliottia was named was Stephen Elliott, 1771-1830, a Yale graduate who wrote *Sketch of the Botany of South Carolina and Georgia*. He added over 1,000 new plants to the known flora of these states.

Joel Poinsett found the *Euphorbia pulcherrima* in the botanical garden in Mexico City and brought it home to South Carolina, where it came to be called poinsettia in his honor. He was our first representative to Mexico in the days before these gentlemen were called ambassadors. He was a plant and garden lover of the first water and planted gardens in at least three places in South Carolina.

plum trees for beauty and fruit

Southern gardeners seem to have forgotten how good plums are in the summer months. A few kinds appear now and then in the grocery stores, but there are many more kinds of fancy or, as the English say, "dessert plums" that we never see. When they are served as dessert in Europe, they are so beautiful that one hardly wants to eat them. 'Green Gage', 'Belle de Louvain', 'Reine Claude', 'Golden Drop', 'Victoria', 'Belgian Purple'—each is a work of art. They look as if they had been painted with water colors. The Europeans are so appreciative of the beauty of these fruits that they pick them by the stem in order not to disturb the beautiful bloom that covers each fruit. They are either served alone or with a light custard—just the right thing for contrast to the acid fruits.

Plums have been cultivated for centuries. The Romans doted on them. In the tenth book of Columella the historian is a description of "the wicker baskets cramm'd with Damask and Armenian and wax plums." Pliny says that there were many varieties of plums in Italy and that the Spanish cultivated them in Andalusia and around Granada. It was a common belief that if plums were grafted upon almond stocks, the fruits would taste like almonds! In those days men were full of fanciful ideas.

There are many species of plums in the world, so it is not surprising that so many varieties came into cultivation. The damson or Damascene plum was brought to Italy from Damascus about 114 B.C., according to Pliny. The Romans brought together all the kinds from the known world of their time.

One of the oldest cultivated plums is said to have been brought to France in the sixteenth century by Queen Claude, wife of Francis I. Of course, varieties are often given different names in different places. The beloved and delicious 'Green Gage' which we still grow today got its name through an accident. The labels fell off some of the new plum trees which the English Gage family ordered from the monastery of Chartreuse in Paris, so the gardener just called the unknown tree 'Green Gage'.

Plum trees are small. They need no more space than a crab apple. The white blossoms come ahead of most of the spring-flowering trees and shrubs, and the plums attract birds from everywhere. Our modern fruit-tree catalogues now offer some decided improvements on the old plums. They are subject to the same brown rot which affects peaches, and we are fortunate now to have varieties that are largely immune, like 'Bruce', 'Methley', 'Shiro', 'Burbank', 'Ozark Premier', 'Bradshaw', 'Santa Rosa', 'Satsuma', 'Fellenberg', and 'Yellow Egg'. Nurseries like Stark Brothers at Louisiana, Missouri 63353, and Bountiful Ridge at Princess Anne, Maryland 21853, list these little trees. Most catalogues tell you which varieties of plums will fertilize each other or whether a variety is self-pollinating. If you have wild plums in your neighborhood they will likely provide the bees with pollen for the earliest cultivated varieties.

delphiniums in the south

The tall blue delphiniums which we admire in pictures of English gardens are difficult to grow in our hot, sticky climate. I gasped the other day when I saw a vase of gorgeous blue delphiniums at the North Carolina Botanical Garden in Chapel Hill. The grower, Dot Wilbur, did not realize what she had accomplished.

After years of trying to grow delphiniums, many southern gardeners have settled for raising them as biennials. But under the best conditions, some of the plants will last for a number of years. These best conditions seem to be a rich, deeply dug, sandy soil with some added lime and a location where plenty of air can pass around the plants. Sunshine for four hours a day is best, but some people are able to raise them in very light shade where there is an hour or so of direct sunshine.

Nowadays, there are many hybrids in seed and perennials catalogues. Most of these are derived from what used to be listed as *Delphinium chinense*. This low, clumpy perennial will stay in most southern gardens if it is not subjected to too much drought. It is easy to grow from seed, which, by the way, require about twenty days to germinate. The Connecticut Yankee delphiniums are low but have spikes of flowers good for cutting. The old Belladonna delphiniums have always been easy to raise as biennials. What has happened to the old Bellamosas, I do not know. They were equally good.

From now till the end of August one can plant delphinium seeds. The earlier you plant, of course, the bigger the plants will be by next spring. Remember, however, the hot days of July and early August. Delphinium babies do not like drought and heat, and you may prefer to await the middle of August before you plant, for germination in early September. Our long autumns allow the plants to develop well before frost.

If you have access to a slat house, the slats will reduce the direct sunshine by one-half, and delphiniums thrive in this situation. They will grow quickly into fine little clumps and flower well when spring comes around. If the plants are not subjected to too much heat and drought, you may pull some of them through several seasons, and the clumps will get bigger and the stems longer each year. The blue flowers of all sorts of delphiniums are well worth the trouble of raising a few plants. Plant several different sorts. Some of the new ones are resistant to the onslaught of mildew—one of the worst enemies of delphiniums. Black spot on the leaves can be controlled by the same chemicals you use for black spot on roses, according to Pat Donofrio, the proprietor of Carroll Gardens in Westminster, Maryland 21157. Pat is a real promoter of fine perennials here in the South. He does not give up on the tough ones! Nor does Mrs. Loleta Powell of Powell's Gardens, Princeton, North Carolina 27569.

august

the signs of late summer

Goldenrods and wild sunflowers, black-eyed Susans and coneflowers are telling us that midsummer is past. In meadows and along streams lavender masses of tall Joe-Pye weed and violet ironweed tower over the gold. There are many species of Joe-Pye weed (*Eupatorium*) scattered from Maine to Florida and from the East to the West Coasts. Cross-country travellers are not seeing the same Joe-Pye everywhere. Ironweeds (*Vernonia*) are numerous, too, some species being quite small. Joe-Pye and ironweed are the signs of late summer.

Pioneer Americans soon learned from the Indians that Joe-Pye roots were medicine. The Indians boiled the roots of this vigorous plant and washed their newborns in the water to give them strength. Some say that if the baby Indian was not strong, the mother might bathe him in Joe-Pye water until he was six years old!

Both the Indians and the white men made a tea out of it for ailments of the genito-urinary tract. The white settlers usually preferred to use a species called boneset for these ailments. Boneset (*E. perfoliatum*), closely akin to Joe-Pye, can be found all through the South and in bloom at the same time. Boneset tea was thought to be beneficial to the knitting of broken bones. The American Indians were animists. They believed that plants and animals had spirits. Since the stems of boneset plants seemed to grow right through the leaves, they thought that boneset tea could penetrate bones and assist the healing process.

The stems of the big Joe-Pye are purple when they emerge in the spring, though some species have spotted stems. Caroline Dormon was especially fond of the new Joe-Pye stems in spring. Her drawings of several of these eupatoriums in *Flowers Native to the Deep South* are particularly beautiful, but then everything Caroline touched was beautiful. Joe-Pye stems get up to seven feet in the coastal plains and hill country, and in the high mountains above three thousand feet they may reach eleven or twelve feet. You cannot miss them even a quarter of a mile away towering over everything else in sight.

Both Joe-Pye and ironweed are easy to grow. They are beautiful and will put up with corners and even thrive behind low shrubbery. A few seeds gathered in September will germinate quickly and give you a fine batch of seedlings. For wettish places, they are just the thing. If we do not begin to grow these native plants, they may vanish from our countryside before we know it. Botanical gardens can provide either seeds or plants or tell you where they can be bought from nurseries that propagate their own plants instead of collecting them from the wild.

late-summer magic

It happened last week! After a long drought, the rains awakened the wonder flowers of late summer: white liriope and blue, tiny *Cyclamen hederifolium*—white and pink—striped spider lilies, and buds of the Sprenger spider lily. All these bring joy to the heart of the gardener tired of drought and summer. Even so, they are but the vanguard of the real magic that is to come in a week or so.

Nothing can light up dark places like the beautiful white liriope— surely one of the choice things of late-summer gardens. Just by itself, this tuberous plant is enough; the grassy foliage is perfect for the white spikes. All through the winter, the leaves cheer up places that do not get much light. Aucubas and liriope are two excellent plants for dark north-facing places in winter. Of course, purple liriope will thrive there too, but the white form is especially stunning.

My little summer cyclamens (*C. hederifolium*) seem to come into bloom earlier and earlier each summer. After the ivy-like leaves die down in May, it is only about two weeks, if there is rain, before they send up a flower or so. Then, until the end of August, they send up more and more, unless there is a drought that slows them down. After August, they cover the ground with pink or white flowers. Grown from seed, these little plants seem to come about 10 percent white. The corms of the white form are more expensive than the pink ones, but they are especially beautiful.

The two well-known physostegias are immensely useful selected varieties of our wild species. Just as the midsummer white form

(*Physostegia virginiana* 'Alba') is going out, the later bright pink and rose kinds take over and carry on till frost. When the main spikes are about to play out, cut them off, feed the plants a little, and water them. In ten days, you will have the beginning of another colorful show. We cannot beat out native plants for good performance.

At the Method Test Gardens of the University of North Carolina at Raleigh in 1974, I saw the new dwarf crape myrtles used most successfully in a new bed of perennials. The charming little plants were then no bigger than a foot tall. They will grow up to a few feet, but they fit beautifully into a flowerbed. Now that they are distributed by southern nurseries, we are all going to like them very much for summer color. They may get killed to the ground in cold areas if you do not give them a little winter protection until they get mature enough stems to withstand low temperatures. With this precaution they will be hardy throughout the South.

green "sallets" unbounded

People have been eating green leaves of all sorts of plants for untold centuries. The Romans seem to have been the greatest greens enthusiasts. Apparently, the cost of precious wheat from North Africa and the lack of fuel to cook their foods influenced the Romans to fill up on salads. We know that they ate every green thing they could find in the British Isles and left a tradition of salad eating behind them.

Modern vegetarians, herb enthusiasts, and promoters of "whole" foods are reviving for us a great many green salad plants from the wilds of Europe and the United States. Seedsmen offer southerners salad plants that stand up to hot, dry weather.

Some greens, like the "rocket" we read about in the old English books of John Parkinson and John Evelyn, are hardly known in America today. Another one popular in Europe is "corn salad." I found seeds of rocket (*Eruca sativa*) in the catalog of J. L. Hudson—P.O. Box 1058, Redwood City, California 94064—who offers also European corn salad as well as the popular lentils.

Corn salad and rocket are fast-growing annuals or biennials that are to be gathered as tender young leaves. Rocket is a relative of turnip greens. Maybe we did not take it on here because it is like our wild cresses that we find ready in fields in the spring.

In England, green "sallets" were called acetaria from their being served, as is done in the South, with vinegar. John Evelyn in 1699 wrote a whole treatise on them called *A Discourse of Sallets*, which was so popular that it ran into numerous printings. If your library will get it for you, you will find it is a delightful little book. Evelyn even gives some recipes and discourses on the great benefits of "sallets" to the world and to his fellow members of the Royal Society.

Last October in London, Joy Larcom made up a salad for the Royal Horticultural Society of lettuce, curled endive, red Italian chicory, Florence fennel, iceplant, rocket, corn salad, winter purslane, salad burnet, sorrel, garden cress, nasturtium leaves, chickweed, hairy bittercress, field pennycress, chopsuey greens, Japanese greens ("Mizuna"), Chinese cabbage, sprouted lentils, mung beans, and rye—all garnished with the flowers of nasturtium, pot marigold, violas, borage, anchusa and *Bellis perennis*! Who says English food is dull or that "they boil everything"?

victorian gardening

As the public turns its interest more and more to the past, some of the lavish Victorian houses are being preserved and Victorian landscaping is reappearing. There is not much danger that there will be fountains and urns in the middle of the front yard again, but some of the more interesting features of the Victorian era have been creeping back into sight for some years.

To understand how it all came about, we need to go back and see what gardeners were doing in Victoria's era. People were intensely interested in the new plants coming to England from all over the world, as they had been for a century or more. Robert Fortune was in China sending back new plants all the time: the winter jasmine, forsythias, wisterias, spireas, weigela. All these new beauties fascinated the English, who grew them at first in greenhouses to be sure they did not kill them out of doors. When Fortune came home, the Royal Horticultural Society sent Theodore Hartweg on his second trip to California. All of the magnificent conifers, as well as new annuals and perennials, were soon growing in English gardens and parks.

Gardeners went plant wild, so to speak. At the big flower shows held by the Royal Horticultural Society, they saw the new plants. Then they bought them from London nurserymen and took them home. It must have been the impact of too many new plants at once that caused them to plant things in every empty space they could find. Up until recently, Americans have not understood how the English can be so interested in their gardens and flowers, but we are rapidly getting that way ourselves. Queen Victoria was so interested in the Horticultural Society of London that she took it under her patronage. After Albert died, she offered to be its president, but her advisors thought it unwise for the monarch to preside over the society.

A typical Victorian garden of the eighteen-thirties and forties was that of Mrs. William Lawrence at Drayton Green near London. The house, full of high windows, looked out upon the lawn filled with little islands of plants. On the grounds were a rustic arch and Cupid, another arch that looked over the paddock, "the Italian walk" with statues at intervals, and a vista with pollarded trees. A tent was sometimes erected at the Cupid arch, and there was also a French parterre with statues, vases, and urns filled with plants. The whole effect was said to be "perfectly dazzling"!

I was in Washington recently with the second-year class of the Landscape Gardening Department of Sandhills College on their field trip. Mr. Jack Monday, Director of the Horticulture Services of the Smithsonian Institute, told us of his plans to redo the grounds around the old Victorian buildings with Victorian flower beds. Figured flower beds, urns, and fountains will be as entertaining now as they were when these buildings were erected. As we left, Mr. Monday asked me what source to go to for Victorian gardening. I suggested *Godey's Lady's Book* from 1835 to the Civil War. It is full of plans, urns, statues, color schemes—and antique stores are full of Victoriana.

some choice summer shrubs

Some of the choicest summer-flowering shrubs happen to grow in our southern bogs. On your way to the beaches, you may see them in places that are often, but not always, flooded. It is very surprising that several of these showy flowering plants will grow in yards and gardens. They do not have to have boggy conditions.

Everybody admires the big evergreen gordonias or loblolly bays (*Gordonia lasianthus*). Most books on native plants will tell you that they are very difficult to cultivate. This is true if you try moving them from the bogs, but there are nurseries where you can buy them in cans or dug from nursery rows. The amazing thing is that loblolly bays can be seen in some yards and gardens up in the hills, growing even in red dirt, where they seem to be perfectly happy. The evergreen leaves of these bays are very handsome and perfectly hardy to our occasional very cold winters here in the South. The camellia-like flowers with golden stamens give away their kinship to camellias, and some camellia gardens have established plants. The bays can take the full sunshine however, so they are in that respect different from their camellia cousins.

I have often sung the praises of the sweet pepperbush (*Clethra alnifolia*), another bog plant that thrives under ordinary conditions in spite of being native to the higher sections of our southern shrub bogs. The clean white spikes of this medium-sized bush are welcome indeed when the daylilies begin to give out in the summer landscape and the earliest crape myrtles get a little washed-out looking. Since pepperbush is accustomed to fires which sweep through the bogs in dry weather, it will come right back if you prune it severely, but it seldom gets over four feet high and fits beautifully into almost any planting. It really is a tough shrub.

Another superb shrub of the bogs is our native titi bush (*Cliftonia monophylla*). The flowers hang down in graceful bunches like sourwood flowers. In fact, titi and sourwood are in the big heath family along with many acid-soil lovers like the azaleas. By this time of year the airy, drooping flowers have turned to green seeds that will eventually turn light brown when fall comes around and the leaves turn partly fiery red and partly green like a big spectacular fern.

Sweet bays are actually trees of the genus *Magnolia* (*M. virginiana*), but in the shrub bogs where fires sweep through and burn the tops off, they keep coming back from roots deep in the peat and as a result seldom become sizeable trees as they do in the true swamps and the yards and gardens where they are allowed to reach maturity. Looking across the bogs, you can tell at once which are the sweet bays because their leaves have silvery undersides which shimmer when the wind blows over the coastal plains.

everybody loves flowers

Everybody loves flowers. If you don't believe it, ride through the towns and villages, through the cities, and out through the country. In the cities, people grow petunias and zinnias even on ash heaps. Where they have no place else, they grow them high up on buildings in window boxes. Out in the country, whole yards are often filled up completely with zinnias, petunias, marigolds, and a riot of other flowers—no grass in these yards—all flowers.

Our summer flowers have come to us from all over the world. European gardens were livened up when the Spanish began bringing the dazzling plants from Mexico and South America to the botanical garden in Madrid. Petunias, zinnias, marigolds—these easy-to-grow annuals caused great excitement all over Europe. The Spanish found that the Aztecs in Mexico and South America were very fond of flowers, which they cultivated in gardens. In one palace garden the flowers were made of gold! These certainly needed only an occasional dusting.

Modern geneticists have worked wonders with the simple little zinnias that were wild in Mexico. A useful new type of zinnia is the low-growing floriferous variety that I saw in one of the All-America test gardens recently. The plants are "stocky," as horticulturists say, and come in all the colors, shades, and tints you could wish.

Dahlias showed up in Madrid in 1789 and were immediately picked up by the French and then shown at the Royal Horticultural Society's show in London in 1803. It seems that they did not know how tender dahlia roots were because the original plants sent to England in 1798 by the Marchioness of Bute had been lost. It is not surprising that it was another English flower lover, the Lady Holland, who sent more tubers in 1804. Dahlias set the gardening world on fire. Societies were organized in almost every country, and big dahlia shows are still popular everywhere. In our southern mountains, the flowers grow as big as dinner plates—if that is any great accomplishment.

Most of the perennial asters that we grow in our gardens are American in origin, as are the showy phloxes. The annual China asters are native to China and Japan. They like a somewhat cool climate and are happiest up in the foothills and mountains.

The popular snow-on-the-mountain is an American wild plant from Minnesota to Texas, and most of the sunflowers of every kind are native plants all over this country. Stokesias are found wild in the Lower South and are evergreen down there where the winters are mild. The brilliant coleuses are said to have originated from a plant cultivated in Java. Not many of us have caught onto the beauties of the hybrid Japanese anemones. They have just started to bloom and are some of the freshest looking things in a garden after the long summer.

Speaking of the long summer, our own native blue *Salvia farinacea* stands right up to the heat and looks good even at the end of a hot summer.

travel notes—hillier's nursery

The long English twilight allowed me to go out and see the beautiful garden in front of Harold Hillier's house, though I had arrived late in the day. First thing to catch the eye was a huge mass of blue and violet agapanthuses waving in the wind. Behind them, some enormous clumps of golden bronze grass (*Stipa gigantea*) were stirring gently. In the past few years, the English have been bringing more and more ornamental grasses from all over the world into their gardens. Some of our southern grasses would really excite them, so I planned to send seeds to Graham Thomas, for it is Graham who has planted the grasses at Wisley for gardeners to enjoy.

Early the next morning, I was out in the dew making notes on the rare trees and shrubs I had seen in the plantings around the Hillier house two years before. I first visited Hillier's in 1954 when the nursery was still in the town of Winchester. At that time I had seen the biggest rose I ever saw, truly a small tree, called 'Arthur Hillier' with big fruits all over it. The catalogue says it has "rose crimson flowers in June-July" and that it was a seedling that occurred in the Hillier nursery in about 1938.

The nursery is now located near Winchester and is the greatest nursery in the world today. Harold Hillier has searched everywhere for the most beautiful plants, from trees to perennials. Their catalogue, *Hillier's Manual of Trees and Shrubs* (Hilliers Nurseries, Ltd., Ampfield House, Ampfield, Romsey, Hants. SO5 9PA England), for which Roy Lancaster was given an award, constitutes one of the most comprehensive lists of ornamental trees and shrubs in existence. What is really amazing is that Hillier's actually can supply all these plants. It may take a year to produce some of the rare ones, but all can eventually be supplied.

A visit to this nursery always emphasizes how very few of the beautiful ornamental plants of the world we are growing here in the southern United States. We seem to be content to grow the same old things, some of them rather poor, while the English and Europeans

struggle to grow beautiful plants from the warmer parts of the world
—that would thrive in our heat.

Harold Hillier is leaving a great legacy to the gardening world by
establishing a big arboretum of rare trees and shrubs, the Hillier
Arboretum. Even in remote places like Sikkim and Manipur, as well as
in our own country, "progress" is destroying beautiful plants as well as
useful ones. It will soon be a fact that these plants must be preserved in
botanical gardens and arboretums so that they can be propagated for
future generations. The botanical gardens which are fortunately springing up in the southern states may soon be the only places where we can
go to get seeds of our own rare plants.

After my visit to Hillier's, I visited Winchester Cathedral and went
back behind the high altar to visit St. Swithin's remains to see if I could
not persuade the rain saint to send a little rain and save England from
eight weeks of drought. Sitting in Westminster Abbey a few days later, I
heard showers on the roof.

more about phloxes

There is no perennial that does any more for summer gardens than
perennial phlox. The many beautiful color phases that have been
selected and developed from this native American meadow plant and
given names as cultivars run into long lists in perennials catalogues.
Around old, abandoned house places and gardens, the purple pink
flowers grow with the weeds and survive even the worst neglect. If the
location is not terribly dry, they will spread from year to year and make
a big show in summer.

It is wise to snip off the heads of your fine kinds of phloxes as the last
flowers open on the heads. If you neglect to do this, seeds will form,
and soon your phlox bed will be full of purplish seedlings that will
crowd out their more beautiful parents. Apparently the seedlings are
stronger than the named cultivars and will starve them out. That is
why none but the purplish ones can usually be found around old places.

Summer phloxes are easy to handle. They need about two square feet
per plant. Since they are essentially meadow plants, drought is their
worst enemy. Though they should be watered once a week during dry
times in summer, do not spray them. Water on the foliage can encourage mildew.

To eliminate mildew on the leaves, you can dust the foliage with sulphur where they are planted in some shade. Weak, summer-strength lime-sulfur (1 part to 60 parts water) will control mildew in the sun. Several kinds of little spots that show up on the foliage are common and not usually very harmful, but if a plant suddenly wilts, dig it out immediately with the surrounding soil and remove it without spilling the soil through the bed.

To get the largest trusses and the biggest show of bloom, many gardeners cut out all the weak stems in late spring. These excellent perennials will respond to water and weak applications of liquid or dry fertilizer up till the time of flowering. When they have bloomed out to the end and begin to play out, clip off the seed heads, do not let them suffer from drought, and the side flowers will make a good showing for you.

Masses of phlox put on the biggest show of the summer flower border. They fit into the middle of the border or as small groups throughout. As free-standing groups of three to five clumps they are really stunning—even right in the edges of the lawn in good soil. The color range of modern phloxes has everything anyone could want. The white cultivars are very desirable in hot summer gardens and will pull together all the loud colors we love.

travel notes—london

The drought in the British Isles and all over Europe this summer [1975] has dried up gardens everywhere. There is little grain in the heads of wheat and other cereals, and the seedless straw is being collected for grazing. In spite of the drought, however, flowers abound in the parks in London and around the great cathedrals. Durham Cathedral, in the North of England, close to Edinburgh, has one of the most dramatic settings in the world. It sits atop a small mountain, and the river almost encircles it in a deep gorge filled with tremendous trees and shrubs—a real arboretum with specimens from all over the world. It is well worth the few hours it takes on the train up from London. Strangely, many English people have never seen it.

"Carpet bedding," so popular in the Victorian era, is to be seen everywhere in Europe today. Grey- and silver-leaved annuals are used as edgers to all sorts of bright annuals in beds, large and small, at the railroad stations, in the parks, and in front of public buildings. At Salisbury Cathedral, a huge bed of annuals had spires of artemisia planted all through it. Was the designer unconsciously influenced by Salisbury Spire—"the highest in all England"?

One of the most popular exhibits at the Royal Horticultural Society's midsummer show for the last several years has been Mrs. Desmond Underwood's "Grey and Silver Plants." Although I had photographed it at several previous shows, I could not resist it again. Her book *Grey and Silver Plants* covers the field. Graham Thomas gave a lecture on perennials the afternoon of the second day of the show. (The occasion brought back happy memories to me of my lecture there in 1954 before the Horticulture Club, presided over by the very gracious Princess Royal.) Several years ago Graham and I sat up till two in the morning checking over American perennials for his forthcoming book. His *Perennial Garden Plants*, with his illustrations, is the only comprehensive book ever published on perennials.

Giant tuberous begonias were a big feature of the flower show. They have now made them so big that one is a little afraid to go near them! The smaller-flowered gladiolas have become very popular, now that "glads" have also reached giant sizes—as big as corn stalks. Reflecting the drought, few delphiniums were in evidence.

Taking the place of delphiniums in the heat, agapanthuses, with those blue-flowered heads that seem to float over the plants, have now become very popular in England and bid fair to compete strongly with delphiniums. I have been trying out every kind of agapanthus I could lay my hands on for years. Today, we have the marvelous Headbourne Hybrids, created by my friend the late Honorable Lewis Palmer, who was honorary secretary of the R.H.S. and who invited me to come see them at his garden near Winchester in 1956. I happened to be in England in 1973 when these hybrids were in the "Trials" at Wisley, and the late Roland Jackman invited me to join in the judging. The beds of these blue and white perennials are still at Wisley and well worth seeing if you go there.

texas flowers

Texas is such a huge state that it is not at all surprising to find a great variety of trees, shrubs, and wild flowers there. Many of them are the same as the plants of the Atlantic seaboard, but in addition there are the plants from their own dry, alkaline plains and the northern and West Texas hills and mountains that are quite different from those of the central and southern parts. In addition to recent floods, upper Texas has terrible droughts.

Even the redbuds vary a lot over such a large area as Texas. In some sections, as you go west, redbuds have smaller, rounded leaves on attractive little rounded trees that are very useful in small yards and restricted places in towns. I have always admired these rounded specimens down there.

Many of the plants from the arid regions of West Texas are armed with thorns and prickles that have protected them from grazing animals. Many also have tiny or fuzzy foliage that holds in the moisture almost as well as cacti do. One of the best known of these is huisache (*Acacia farnesiana*), that blooms in later winter or very early spring. Huisache was once grown in Charleston and southward, as was noted by Tom Jefferson. People picked the little fragrant, fuzzy balls and carried them around in their handkerchiefs. Even the gentlemen are said to have done this. Today, I know of only one small tree of huisache (pronounced wee-satch) that has survived in Charleston, where it was called apopanax.

There are plants in the Big Bend of the Rio Grande that grow nowhere else in the world. Best known of all these is what gardeners are apt to call the pink yucca (*Hesperaloe parviflora*). We are lucky these days to be able to buy this fascinating plant in cans from our plant stands and nurseries. From a bunch of upright, yucca-like foliage arise several three- to six-foot stems, and in later spring, tiny flame-colored bells hang from the arching stems.

Hesperaloe is extremely drought resistant. It will grow up against buildings where no water ever gets to it and where the lime from foundations and walkways makes the soil very alkaline. The flowers are produced almost without ceasing from spring till fall. While they do not make a gaudy show, they are extremely pleasing all summer long in almost impossible places.

Of all the wild flowers native to Texas, the best known, of course, are the Texas bluebonnets (*Lupinus subcarnosis*), which we have learned to grow in our gardens here in the East. After many trials, we have discovered how to get them to germinate. After the seedbed is prepared, roll it down flat. Then scatter the seeds over the surface and mash them down firmly with a board. Do not bury then, but a light scattering of pine needles may be sprinkled over them to keep rains from eroding the bed. Lime should be included in the seedbed soil, and a beans or peas culture may be shaken in with the seeds before planting.

I recently had a week's visiting with Texas plant lovers which was a feast of enthusiasm. Back in the twenties and thirties, I discovered the wonders of Texas flowers and was even invited to give a lecture at Denton on, of all things, Texas wild flowers! Many of these fascinating plants will soon be coming into nurseries.

figs

August and September are the months when southerners enjoy big crops of figs (*Ficus carica*), those heavenly fruits so beloved down through the ages. Someone has said that people are divided into two groups: those who are inordinately fond of figs and those who do not care for them at all.

Fig lovers, however, consider themselves a superior class because of the famous men who have so dearly loved this ancient fruit. The prophet Mahomet is credited with saying that if he should wish a fruit brought to Paradise it would certainly be the fig. While Eve's "apple " of temptation might have been any of several fruits, her fig-leaf skirt could not have been from any other tree. How comforting it is to find one definitely identifiable tree all through the Old Testament story! The Athenians, it is said, loved figs so greatly that they forbade their export to other countries. Citizens who informed on fig exporters sometimes told malicious lies about innocent people. Informers were called *sykophantai* from two Greek words meaning discoverer of figs. Our word *sycophant* today means informer, parasite, liar, flatterer, imposter—or used to. Of course, the Romans, who had the best of everything, were great cultivators and lovers of figs. Saturn, one of the Roman deities, is represented wearing a crown of figs, and Romulus and Remus are pictured being suckled by their wolf mother underneath a fig tree. By the time of Pliny, there were twenty-nine kinds of figs in cultivation. He says, ". . . figs are restorative and the best food that can be taken by those who are brought low by long sickness, and are on the recovery. They increase the strength of young people, preserve the elderly, and make them look younger, and with fewer wrinkles. They are so nutritive as to cause corpulency and strength: for this cause, professed wrestlers and champions were in times past fed with figs."

Southerners can grow figs so easily that it is surprising that there are not more of them. No one who likes them need be without them. Even when these trees are completely neglected, they seem to survive both starvation and drought. Around old smokehouses and chimneys in the country, fig bushes abound. The commonest variety seems to be the little sweet "Spanish" fig, so often made into preserves. 'Brown Turkey' is a big luscious variety that is a little more sensitive to cold. 'Green Ischia' from the Island of Ischia off the coast of Italy, is the hardy fig.

hot-weather dangers

In very hot weather—especially during droughts—shrubbery is in danger of red-spider damage. Boxwood is especially subject to these little mites that seem to delight in dense evergreens. Conifers can be damaged, too, before you know it. In hot, dry places, creeping junipers are very subject to attack. In front of hot buildings, Pfitzer junipers are vulnerable.

Spider mites etch the leaves of broadleaf evergreens and leave the foliage with a grey green, sickly look. If you examine a leaf with a hand lens, you will see that it looks as if it had been scratched with a pin. The needles of conifers turn partly brown.

The simple, old-fashioned practice of spraying conifers and broadleafs once a week with very strong water pressure is very effective in holding down the population of spider mites. Go over each shrub carefully, being sure to spray down inside the bush and to wash off every little spider web. Before you start, clean out the debris that has collected down inside each shrub. When wet weather returns with the autumn rains, the spiders will diminish, but you should still keep up with them by watching for their tiny webs.

During the wet, sticky weather of late summer in the South, boxwoods are very subject to Volutella blight. It kills whole sections of the bushes right to the ground. The leaves turn yellow, and then you discover the characteristic salmon-colored pustules on the branches inside. Clean out the bushes thoroughly right now and spray them with 1 to 50 lime-sulfur. This is an old-fashioned spray made from water and the powder that you can get from the seed or plant store. Follow the directions for the weak, summer-strength dilution because strong sulfur damages plants in the hot summer sun. Lime-sulfur is not harmful to birds.

Pachysandra is also somewhat subject to Volutella blight. You will find brown blotches on the leaves and the salmon-colored pustules on the stems. Bordeaux Mixture, another old-fashioned spray, is the one recommended for it. Use only half the amount indicated on the label. It pays to inspect all your plants and shrubs during the very hot weather.

september

peony-planting time

The much-needed rains of late August and early September awakened in my woods the early colchicums and stimulated more and more buds to arise and open on the beds of *Cyclamen hederifolium*. Some early red spider lilies surprised me and sent up their naked stalks and fire-red flowers. The cardinal flowers had already tried to open in the drought, and the white bracts on mountain mints were showing. The white spider lilies must have had their leaves damaged by the late cold last spring because not a one has bloomed so far.

It is time to order peonies and get the soil ready for September planting. We southerners have had bad luck with the big, heavy, bomb types of peonies; they cannot open in the sudden hot spells of spring this far south. The coolest location on your property is the best for all kinds of peonies below Mason and Dixon's line. People can grow beautiful peonies, however, and they are a joy where they can flower normally. Back in 1938 I had an illustrated article in *House Beautiful* magazine recommending the early single and Japanese peonies. Now in the eighties, I will say it again: the singles and the Japanese peonies flower well ahead of the big heavy kinds and will open in southern gardens. They are light and airy, and many gardeners prefer them in the landscape.

Planting a peony is like planting an apple tree. They each live for more than a human lifetime. Gardeners must take this fact into account when they prepare the soil for any kind of peony. It is a big, woody-rooted perennial—a sort of deciduous shrub. In the cooler parts of our country, there are peonies that have been in gardens for three or more generations. This fact is enough to inspire anyone to prepare the soil carefully for such a long-time treasure. Old clumps may bear as many as one hundred flowers! In good soil and where properly fed, they go on almost indefinitely before needing to be divided.

Since the roots spread out and go down into the soil for some distance from the big thick main roots, the hole for a single plant should be dug two feet or more deep and three feet square. All the ordinary soil should be removed and replaced with the best garden soil available, into which a teacupful of fine bone meal and another teacupful of coarse bone meal should be mixed. If you can get hold of some crushed oyster shell, add another teacupful of that, too! The coarse bone meal and oyster shell will decay slowly and supply for years the phosphorus so needed by all deep-root plants. A topdressing with 8-8-8 once a year before the leaves emerge will supply the necessary potash and nitrogen. Actually, you do not need the middle 8 if you have incorporated bone meal in the soil, but it is sometimes hard to find fertilizer like 8-2-8. Old-fashioned gardeners top-dressed their peonies with some wood ashes for the potash and some cow manure for the nitrogen.

Peonies are extremely sensitive about the depth of their buds. They must be exactly two inches below the surface after the plants have settled in the soil. To accomplish this, put a board across the hole and hold the root cluster with one hand at the proper level while you fill in the soil with the other hand. Pack the soil down tight (you may use your feet) and be sure that the buds are just two inches down!

colchicums

Masses of weeds and wild flowers were growing over the beds of fall-flowering bulbs when I arrived home from a trip to England. Down into the woods I went with my tools, and over the beds in a hurry, cutting away as closely as I dared. Any day now—any hour—the colchicums would be coming up. Sure enough, the very next day they began to awaken from their summer sleep! I had been just in time.

Like small, lavender tulips with white stems, the colchicums erupt in bunches from the dry earth in late August and early September. They are so fresh and so promising of fall flowers to come that, once you have them in your garden, you will watch eagerly for them every year. The white "stems" of colchicum flowers are not really stems at all but elongated parts of the flowers themselves, as are the "stems" of winter-flowering irises. All of these fragile flowers must be put into small containers when you cut them for the house. They will last only a few days in water, but you can bring in fresh ones every day or so.

More and more of the fine named colchicums are appearing in seed stores and nurseries. If you can, buy 'The Giant', which has the biggest flowers. It blooms in the early days of September. 'Autumn Queen' is deep, bright violet and flowers first of the named colchicums. There are several with French names, which come in very subtle shades of violet and pink. Some are named for poets. Last in the season to bloom—as late as November, among the fallen leaves—is 'Lilac Wonder'. This one has many small flowers. Blooming sometimes with 'Lilac Wonder', sometimes even later, is the double 'Water Lily'. You will not believe it when you see its small white flowers appearing after hard frost. They are expensive bulbs but worth the price.

Colchicums like southern gardens. They thrive in good soil with little or no care at all. Do not be alarmed when you see the corms sticking out of the ground. Even if you plant them with two inches of soil over the top of the bulb, they are likely to come up and push their noses out. They may even get washed out onto the top of the ground with no harm.

Colchicum foliage does not appear until the late winter. Frost and cold do not bother the new leaves, which will develop into big green rosettes, beautiful in themselves. They expand into large bunches and mature and die down with the daffodil leaves in late spring.

Colchicums are not crocuses though many people confuse the two. They are bigger and have large leaves. Squirrels will not eat the corms, and rabbits will not eat the foliage. Keep the colchicum corms away from small children because they contain a poisonous drug. Plant them as soon as you get them.

september in the south

September in the South is still summertime. The sun seems more penetrating than ever, but up in the hills and in the mountains it is chilly at night.

This is the time of orange pyracantha berries and 'Heavenly-Blue' morning-glories. The orange-berried pyracanthas are not hurt by winter cold as the red-berried kinds can be. Long wands of yellow and orange and terra-cotta berries are brightening up yards and gardens now. For a while, it seemed that people would no longer plant these yellow and orange types—they were so taken by the red-berried ones when they came onto the market in the hill country thirty years ago. Happily, there are still a lot of orange kinds around to contrast with the morning-glories.

In the nurseries, you will find several colors or hues in the early coloring varieties—from light yellow to deep terra-cotta. Since pyracanthas are notoriously difficult to move in big sizes, buy small ones or get them in cans. Even in cans, the berries will be colored up now so that you can tell what you are getting. Also, they will transplant with no trouble at any size when grown this way.

Nothing is more beautiful in September than the snowy white, sweet clematis (*Clematis paniculata*) that fills the meadows and people's yards and gardens. Nothing is easier to grow, either. In fact, this little vine can be a nuisance and come up in places where it is not wanted so that it sometimes winds up on the dump heap. However, we are not using it as effectively in the landscape as we could. The other day, I saw a white festoon of clematis draped gracefully from one side of a hemlock. I recalled that I had been struck by the delicate beauty of another one of these little vines on a Colorado spruce in Shreveport. The stiffness of the spruce provided a striking contrast to the airiness of the clematis. If you ever see it climbing around in a late-flowering crape myrtle, you will probably rush home and snatch it off your dump heap and start it up your own shrub. Some of the old-fashioned purple crape myrtles do not flower until late, and their violet tones are delightful with white. In case you do not like vines in trees, you can plant it nearby on a fence or post where the two will be seen close together.

In meadows and low places all over the South, our little wild clematis (*C. virginiana*) is in bloom now. The greenish white clouds of flowers look something like *C. paniculata*, but the flower masses are not so white.

japanese pagoda trees

Visitors to Longwood, the beautiful Du Pont gardens at Kennett Square, Pennsylvania, often want to know what the gorgeous big trees are that "look like big ferns." These old Japanese pagoda trees would be worth going to Longwood to see if there were no gardens there at all. We have a few of these trees in the southern states, planted as far back as the beginning of the century when they were sold by my family nursery, the old Lindley Nursery in Greensboro, North Carolina, and by the Fruitland Nursery in Augusta, Georgia.

By now these trees, planted in cemeteries and on estates, are up to fifty feet tall. In full leaf, they look rather like black locusts, but they flower later, in early summer. Strangely, in winter their bark and configuration make them resemble oaks! The botanical name for these splendid shade trees is *Sophora japonica*. The Japanese got credit for them, but they are really Chinese, like so many "Japanese" trees. A French monk, Father D'Incarville, sent seeds of the pagoda tree back to France in 1747. The Chinese baked the flowers and buds in an oven until crisp to make a yellow dye for their silks. Perhaps the "natural dyes" people will want to try them. Chinese Wilson mentions the pagoda tree all through his travel books on China. Although they do not grow fast, they are strong and resistant to wind and sleet storms. Many of the nurseries in the North, as well as a few southern nurseries, offer them.

The age of several pagoda trees in Europe attests to their longevity. There is a big specimen in Kew Gardens in London, planted in 1760. When it was measured back in 1914, the trunk was 13 feet around. Visitors to the famous rose garden at Versailles at the Petit Trianon always admire the specimen there. There is also a huge tree at the Schoenbrunn Botanic Garden near Vienna. Sometime before 1844, it was found to be 48 feet tall with a spread of 55 feet. When measured again about 1914, it was 18 feet in girth and some 70 feet tall.

The white flowers, carrying a hint of yellow, of this sophora have a beautiful way of falling off all at once onto the ground so as to make it look like a light snow has fallen in summer. The seedpods are small beans with the seeds swollen out. They look like small necklaces. Inside, there is a sticky substance that could be used for glue. You can hardly get it off your fingers!

southern maples

The southern states, from Maryland to Texas, are blessed with gorgeous maples of several different species. In the higher areas, the sugar maple (*Acer saccharum*) has just finished its dazzling show of colors. Lower down in the piedmont and coastal plains, our red maples (*A. rubrum*) are still showing off. In the spring, the flowers of sugar maples turn the trees into light gold while those of the red maples range from rust to blood red. On the edges of swamps, when these flowers are ablaze, they are a fine contrast to the black water and grey spanish moss.

There are many variations in our native maples. A tree in the yard of Inez Conger at Arcadia, Louisiana, has very large leaves with an extra lobe and wonderful coloration. This one is much like the Carolina red maple around the old University of North Carolina in Chapel Hill. Its leaves are very broad, with five lobes!

The gorgeous Drummond maple, a variety of the red maple, was named for Thomas Drummond who is said to have discovered it on a botanical trip early in the last century. The many color variations of this swamp-forest tree have been under study at Southwestern Louisiana University where Dr. James Foret has selected especially beautiful types. Even though the Drummond maple grows in low areas, it succeeds in good soil in cultivation in yards and gardens.

Because of their rapid growth, trees of the native silver maple (A. *saccharinum*) were once planted all over the South. Alas, speed is not everything! Silver maples break up easily in sleet storms, and they turned out to be especially subject to the San Jose scale when it hit the South from California. When I was a child, I hated the scale on the branches when I climbed up into one of these trees.

There are several other interesting native maples. The southern sugar maple (A. *floridanum*) has rather simple leaves, and the black maple (A. *nigrum*), extremely pointed leaves of a very dark green. The white-barked sugar maple (A. *saccharum* ×*leucoderme*) is almost a bush that occurs in a few places in the South. Although some people dislike the little box elder (A. *negundo*), it is really a beautiful small tree with a great deal of character. Most people do not recognize it—with its three leaflets to the stem—as a maple at all, but the long hanging bunches of winged maple seeds give it away right off. The need for small trees these days will soon bring it into its own. There is a beautiful little green-barked maple known as the striped maple (A. *pennsylvanicum*), common in the mountains, that is a very attractive small tree.

If you wish to study southern maples, read William Coker and Henry Totten, *Trees of the Southeastern States*. It is out of print but in most libraries all over the South. Claitor's Book Store, (Box 239, Baton Rouge, Louisiana 70821) has Dr. Clair Brown's *Louisiana Trees and Shrubs*. These well-illustrated books will be a constant joy.

september-sown annuals and perennials

The spectacular show which we southern gardeners can get from certain September-sown annuals and perennials is so great that I like to remind everybody—with monotonous regularity—of the rewards of September seed sowing.

Our long, beautiful, open weather from now till Christmas gives ideal conditions for the growth of hardy annuals and some perennials. This is especially true of the spring-flowering annuals. No bigger show can be had for such little effort. Chinese forget-me-nots come up at once and begin to make beautiful rosettes of foliage which are cheerful in the winter garden and increasingly so as spring comes on. Then, these well-established plants just try themselves when warm weather comes along.

If you did not sow *Anchusa italica* in June it is well worth planting right now. Planted in the fall, it will usually bloom the following spring, but if not, it will brighten up the spring garden with deep blue every year from then on. In summer, the foliage dies down completely when the first drought comes along, but this gives more room for summer perennials. The winter foliage is fuzzy and beautiful until hard frosts.

The Shirley poppies (*Papaver rhoeas*) dote on our fall weather and mild winters. If you sow them now, you will have them in full blast in the spring garden. Love-in-a-mist is so feathery that you can scatter it over almost the whole spring garden without interfering with anything. It is even lighter than larkspur in effect.

There are so many sophisticated kinds of larkspur these days that we need not weep too many tears over the difficulties of delphiniums in the South. The pure blues, whites, and pinks of the single- as well as the double-flowered varieties will please you if you have never grown them.

For the yellows and oranges in the spring garden, one can hardly beat the California poppies (*Eschscholtzia californica*). The delicate foliage would be a thing of beauty in itself in the winter garden even if the plants never had a flower on them. The cheerful yellow flowers begin to bloom in the late winter.

If you do not have Johnny-jump-ups (*Viola tricolor*) as friendly little weeds in your garden, a few seeds sown now will produce their elfin glee when March comes again.

The California annual *Nemophyla menziesii* called Baby-Blue-Eyes will succeed in southern gardens if you plant it in September. The little sky-blue flowers are extremely attractive. When the heat of our mid-spring hits this little plant, it usually burns right up, but it flowers in late winter and goes on for several weeks into the spring. When the plants wilt, just pull them up and plant some other annual.

arboretums and botanical gardens

Arboretum and botanical garden are words that have begun to appear in print more often than formerly. Since there seems to be a lot of confusion about their application, we might examine their meaning and use. An arboretum is simply a collection of trees. A botanical garden is usually a collection of all kinds of plants, and the larger ones have enough trees to be at the same time arboretums.

In this country, perhaps the most famous arboretum is the Arnold Arboretum in Boston, affiliated with Harvard University. It has a magnificent collection of trees from all over the world. In winter, the conifers are gorgeous. They have made an attempt to collect all the conifers of the world that can be grown in the northern states. It has also some of the finest flowering trees and shrubs from all parts of the world. Most famous are the plants collected by Chinese Wilson. One of Wilson's greatest finds, as far as we in the South are concerned, was the regal lily, a wonderful performer for us in the cooler parts of Dixie. Wilson broke his leg on the occasion of the discovery of this lily.

I have for many years been deeply engaged in the promotion of botanical gardens in the southern states. The late Mrs. Will Lake and I shared this interest back in the thirties, and she succeeded in getting the Fort Worth Botanical Garden established. By hammering away at the old University of North Carolina since 1927, we finally established the North Carolina Botanical Garden and the Hunt Arboretum which is to be a part of this very large garden. Happily, I had a finger in the establishment of the Tennessee Botanical Garden and Fine Arts Center in Nashville. More recently, the honor fell to me to assist with the birth of the Georgia Botanical Garden at Athens and to dedicate the Barnwell Art and Garden Center in Shreveport. Interested citizens of Asheville, North Carolina, have established a beautiful botanical garden, so we are on the way!

When the city fathers of one of our southern cities were turned down by a new industry, they were told, "Why, you do not even have a botanical garden." "What is that?" enquired one of the fathers! Now they know—and they have one.

colchicums and fall crocuses

The big fat corms of colchicums and the tiny flat corms of autumn crocuses are in the stores now. What an exciting time it is! The colchicums will be in bloom in a few weeks. If you forget to plant them, they will bloom anyway—dirt or no dirt—right on the shelf or in the bag they came in.

There is always something of a dilemma in gardener's minds as to where to plant these autumn beauties in the garden or on the grounds. When they like their location and have enough food to sustain them, they will go on for a long time before you have to divide them. Just stuck anywhere with no regard to their needs, they may disappear after one or two seasons.

Colchicums can be planted shallow. Only an inch or so of soil need cover the big corms. The soil must be fairly rich, however. They are like tulips in that they have tiny, fragile, short roots that do not range more than a few inches from the corms. Therefore, they must have food in their soil which will be available in late winter and early spring when the huge leaves come up and start to build up those numerous flowers they produce in autumn.

Since both crocuses and colchicums have small, delicate flowers, they are at their best planted near walks or paths, and of course should never be hidden at the back of a bed. They should be where they can be enjoyed intimately—on the sitting terrace they can be with you for many hours of the day. They will cheer up the front of perennial plantings in September and October, but do not plant the corms closer than two feet from strong-rooted perennials. They are exceptionally beautiful with Japanese anemones because the flowers of each come in like shades.

Since all crocuses can be planted as deep as six inches—if the soil is rich for another four inches beneath that—they can be planted almost anywhere and will survive when you work over their tops. Some crocuses in an old garden of mine are still going after twenty-five years. One would really have to dig deeply to find them now because they work their way down in the earth.

Crocuses are especially beautiful at the foot of a rock. Their grassy

"The cheery fall crocuses are a great joy anywhere you plant them. . . ."

leaves come on in autumn and, like the spider lilies, need winter sunshine. Christmas ferns and ebony spleenwort are splendid companions for them. The cheery fall crocuses are a great joy anywhere you plant them, however. *Crocus longiflorus* does not flower till the leaves are all down, at a time when bloom is especially welcome.

Rabbits eat crocus foliage, but a little fence no more than eighteen inches high will keep them out or, if you dislike fences, a little dried blood will keep them away, too. Rabbits are "chicken hearted."

after a cold winter

A great many plants were as much as two weeks late in flowering this year after the cold, cold winter. Winters seem to be actually getting colder. Our normal "warm spells" have not ceased, but the cold ones are more vigorous.

Last winter was a rough one on red spider lilies (*Lycoris radiata*). The early kind showed only a single flower in my garden in August. The common one that usually blooms in September has not yet shown any blooms at all. If yours have not flowered at all up until now, you may still lift the bulbs and separate them if you will be careful not to destroy the roots and if you replant them the same day they are dug. A year when there are no blooms is your big chance to divide them. Don't forget that they like bone meal!

The reason for the lack of bloom this September lies in the fact that their foliage was badly damaged last winter and spring when they would normally be making bulb growth and storing up energy for summer buds and flowers. In protected places and warm spots, they will be all right and will flower. They will not bloom much above Washington, D.C. Baltimoreans are ecstatic when they can get even a few flowers in September. They fuss over the winter leaves and protect them in an all-out effort to bloom the bulbs each year. They even think it worthwhile to import the bulbs annually to get a few flowers. My friend Ernie Jenkins has been testing them there for me for years.

No bloom has appeared yet on the little yellow "fall daffodils" (sternbergias) either. Some foliage is showing, and I expect the flowers pretty soon. Sternbergias are more resistant to cold than red spider lilies. Gardeners on Long Island grow them with some protection for the evergreen foliage. The big bulb dealers who advertise in the national flower magazines now carry *Sternbergia lutea*. Get their catalogues if you want this delightful, golden yellow crocus-like flower in your garden every year, and if you cannot find the bulbs in your favorite seed stores.

I promoted sternbergias for so many years to Shreveport gardeners that Mr. Campbell, the director of the Barnwell Art and Garden Center, decided to give sternbergia bulbs away free to gardeners who attended a symposium on autumn-flowering bulbs which was held there. Back in the thirties I introduced them on Lookout Mountain above Chattanooga, where they have thrived and multiplied for years now.

Colchicums, the "meadow-saffron," have bloomed all right this year. Their foliage is extremely winter hardy. It comes up in big bunches long before the daffodils have sent up their leaves in spring. Their hardiness to cold and the fact that rodents will not eat colchicum corms make these bulbs very desirable.

the wild asters

Every single one of the wild asters native to the southern states is a beautiful perennial worth growing in our gardens. Most of the soil in which our roadside asters are struggling along is so very poor that we seldom see these glorious flowers in their natural size and condition.

Thirty-five to forty species and subspecies are growing in our woods and fields, bogs and swamps. If you want to grow perennials which are drought-proof, disease-proof, and showy, then asters are the gems of the autumn for you, along with wild sunflowers and goldenrod. Their colors run from pure white through the lavenders to deep violet. Most of them are big perennials that stay small until late summer. They do not interfere with the spring perennials since they do not spread out over these plants until after the spring bloom is finished.

The very best way to acquaint yourself with the wild asters is to take a walk out into the woods and fields right now before the frost gets them. Remember that only where the soil is fairly rich will you see the asters in their natural condition. When you take them into your garden, they will grow to their full size and dazzle you with their brilliance.

The Europeans fell in love with American asters back as far as the time when the elder John Tradescant in London was establishing his museum of natural history, then called Tradescant's Ark. John Tradescant the younger came to Virginia in 1637, 1642, and 1654 and took home many plants to grow in King Charles's gardens. In the Tradescants' honor, an aster was named (*Aster tradescantii*), as was the genus that includes Virginia spiderwort (*Tradescantia virginiana*) and its close kin, wandering Jew (*T. fluminensis*).

The Michaelmas daisies of our gardens come from selections of the New York aster introduced to England as long ago as 1710. Perhaps the best-known cultivar of this plant is the good old aster 'Climax', which Graham Thomas in his book on perennials describes as spode in color. Then there are innumerable old, named varieties in our gardens—all worthwhile, tall, autumn flowers.

White-topped, heart-leaved, stiff-leaved, starved, southern smooth, rush, narrow-leaved, smooth are some of the identifying names, reflecting the Latin names, of our wild asters. Their Latin names often describe them well, but we shall some day enjoy these splendid plants and take them into our gardens and give them distinguishing common names.

goldenrod

The great sheets of goldenrods on our highways and in fields and woods at this time of the year are amazingly various. If you will study them a bit, you will see surprising differences between the species. Besides the many variations in size and shape, there are even some species that are white—not golden at all—and some look just like asters! Nature has provided a goldenrod for just about every type of place you can think of. There is even a species that grows in salt water. Several kinds grow in very wet and low places, some grow on hard, rocky banks, and a few inhabit shady woods.

The two fragrant goldenrods are the favorites of some woods and fields lovers. One is Chapman's goldenrod (*Solidago chapmanii*), named for a southern botanist. The other species is *S. odora*, which smells of anise; a big surprise when you bruise the leaves. One of my favorite goldenrods is called blue-stem (*S. caesia*). It is the delicacy of this one—just the opposite of most of the species—that is so attractive. Right now, it can be found in woods—sometimes in deep shade— waving its graceful wands of gold in the breezes. People just learning the wild flowers are usually surprised to find that there is a spring goldenrod. This species is *S. verna*. It is one of the relatively few yellow late-spring wild flowers.

When the search was on during the last world war for sources of natural rubber, my friend the late B. Y. Morrison, director of the National Arboretum in Washington, tested almost everything in our flora. He found that the big goldenrod that grows in moist and wet places along our roads had the highest rubber content. It was not then a practical source, but maybe someday a geneticist will develop it for this use.

In European catalogues of perennials, there are several named cultivars of goldenrod. If you will take any of our wild ones into your garden, you will be surprised at the way it responds to the least bit of good soil and food. The goldenrod already growing along your woodlands and driveways will respond quickly to a handful of fertilizer.

some odd trees

A number of odd trees are to be found here and there over the South, some of them favorites in Victorian times. The Chinese parasol tree (*Firmiana simplex*), the cut-leaf and the weeping beeches, the weeping mulberry (grafted on a straight mulberry), the monkey puzzle tree (*Araucaria imbricata*), the Japanese pagoda tree (*Sophora japonica*), and the Caucasian wing-nut tree (*Pterocarya fraxinifolia*) were among those often planted in the middle of the lawn! In more recent times, tree lovers have planted specimens of the dove tree (*Davidia involucrata*), the sawtooth oak (*Quercus acutissima*), the ruby horse-chestnut (*Aesculus rubicunda*), and the new hybrid chestnuts.

Old cemeteries and parks are the places to look for the parasol tree. You cannot miss it; the trunk is bright green on all but the oldest parts. The huge leaves are the shape of maple leaves, and at this time of year, the trees carry big, loose whorls resembling miniature boats with pea-like seeds, usually two on one side of the "boat" and three on the other side. These were one of the delights of my childhood. Our big, green-trunked parasol tree was easy to climb. It stood over a Victorian fountain, which is now in my own garden, and the two-inch-long boats with the little pea-men on each side fell from the parasol tree and floated in the pool around the fountain.

The cut-leaf beeches and weeping mulberries have long since gone out of style, but they have outlasted *Godey's Lady's Book*, and some huge specimens are still to be found in the oldest cemeteries. "Tent caterpillars" (really the fall web-worm) by this time of year have long since feasted on the leaves of the weeping mulberry and destroyed most of them. Only a few monkey puzzles are left in the Gulf area and Florida. The Caucasian wing-nut tree was once popular as a "fast-growing tree." So was the Siberian elm (*Ulmus pumila*), but it broke up badly in ice storms, and most of the forms that came from seed were short-lived and had such soft inner bark that sapsuckers "ate them up" in a few seasons. Don Wyman of the Arnold Arboretum says in *Trees for American Gardens* that 'Coolshade', a variety carried by nurseries in the Midwest, is an improved form. We southerners must get from California the "evergreen" form of the tiny-leaved Chinese elm (*U. parvifolia*), which is a handsome elm indeed.

The sawtooth oak, which has been planted here and there, is not one of my favorites because the long, stiff, thick leaves stay on all winter. Most of the dove trees in the South are still too young to flower, but they are an unbelievable sight when the trees are covered with "white doves" or "handkerchiefs." This was one of Chinese Wilson's favorites. We really ought to be enjoying the beauty of the small ruby horse-chestnut because one of its parents was our red buckeye (*Aesculus pavia*). European cities have planted these dense, smallish trees extensively. The Madrone of the Pacific Coast and the European strawberry tree are being tried out in the gardens of a number of southern connoisseurs of trees.

october

october in charleston

Charleston is a gardener's delight in October and November. It is then cool enough to walk up and down the streets, peeking through fences at the little gardens, some of them tiny. Gardeners from the hill country feel a little envious when they see masses of coral vine (*Antigonon leptopus*) ramping over fences and tall shrubs. Up here in the hills, we have to cover the tubers deep in mulch in winter or take them into the basement to prevent their freezing. Coral vine became very popular back in the thirties (there was also a white form), but people forgot to mulch the roots, and one seldom sees the beautiful coral or white fringes any more.

The loquats (*Eriobotrya japonica*) in Charleston are enough to make hill gardeners very envious. Only in really protected places can we of the Middle and Upper South keep them permanently. They may last even twenty or thirty years in unprotected places, but some extreme winter is apt to kill them back. The fruits are a delight, and the autumn flowers scent the air with a perfume like no other.

Some of the walls of the buildings in the little gardens are covered with the delicate-leaved fig vine (*Ficus pumila*). It is a softer green and has a finer texture than ivy. Where it has climbed high, it sends out its fruiting limbs with the little, green "figs" on them. This evergreen vine is barely hardy to the cold in much of the "up-country," but if it gets killed to the ground, it will spring up again and grow several feet in one summer.

The stroller in the streets is delighted by the scent of the ginger lilies (*Hedychium coronarium*). This is a spicier odor than that of the loquats. Ginger lilies look like delicate cannas. It is hard to believe that the flowers can produce so much fragrance. In greenhouses and conservatories, we see many relatives of this plant with yellow and red flowers, but the simple, white-flowered ones are delightful and much more fragrant than their hothouse relatives. Up in the hills, many old gardens have ginger lilies. Even farther up into cold country, the plants can be brought through the winter by deep mulches under boxes placed over the clumps. These fragrant-flowered plants are closely akin to the ginger which enlivens our foods so greatly.

Ah, but it is the old tea roses that enchant the visitor to the "Low Country" in October and November, from Charleston and Savannah to Mobile and New Orleans. In old gardens, little and big, in cemeteries and down alleys and climbing up on shanties and shacks, the old tea roses have been hanging on, awaiting their rescuers.

autumn and eleagnus

Falling leaves and musky fragrance bespeak southern autumn days. Now comes the delicious odor of elaeagnus bushes just as the nights get cooler and the days are full of sunshine. Mockingbirds respond with bursts of song. They must like the cooler days.

Elaeagnus is a relative newcomer amongst the scents beloved of southern gardeners. Called Russian olive, it is from a group of evergreen and nonevergreen shrubs which bear tiny odoriferous flowers. Some kinds flower in the autumn and some in spring. The cultivated evergreen ones are some of our handsomest shrubs. Because of their habit of sending out long growths each year these bushes are sometimes spurned. Their fall fragrance, however, has made gardeners willing to prune back the big growths once a year and keep them from becoming far-climbing scramblers. They are not true climbers since they do not twine. The young spurs that stick out from the leaf axils act as hooks, and when the long growths go up into a tree, the hooks hold. Neither the wind nor a strong man can dislodge them.

The evergreen elaeagnuses come from Japan, where botanists describe their fall fragrance as like that of gardenias. They produce their tiny, fragrant flowers for weeks and weeks. They are a big help because they mask the musky, unpleasant odor of *Camellia sasanqua*, which blooms at the same time. The way to get the most out of an elaeagnus is to plant it underneath a big shade tree and let it go up the tree. In the fall, the scent will descend onto yards and gardens in the whole vicinity.

In cultivation they make many seeds, with the resulting development of numerous cultivars or varieties, now to be found in southern catalogues. The old Fruitland Nurseries of Augusta, Georgia, and the Lindley Nurseries of Greensboro, North Carolina, introduced them to the public back in the twenties and before. I recall what great thickets they made in the nurseries when a block of them was left alone and not dug for even as short a time as two or three years. It took a bulldozer to remove them. We have the old Fruitland Nurseries to thank for the named cultivar *Elaeagnus pungens* 'Fruitlandii'. This gorgeous evergreen has silvery undersides to its leaves and has many more flowers than any other kind.

evergreen ferns

After the leaves are down and the autumn winds have settled them into their permanent places, the evergreen ferns cheer gardeners and nature lovers with myriad filmy fronds. Deep woods that have not been taken over by Chinese honeysuckle usually boast patches of green Christmas fern (*Polystichum acrostichoides*), here and there. In older forests, whole carpets of it can be found in cool, moist places with a northern exposure.

It is really hard to understand why we have not taken to Christmas ferns more than we have. They are easy to transplant in winter or early spring, and they will brighten up dark corners where almost nothing else will grow. All of the wild ferns thrive and multiply in the garden if they have the right exposure.

A section of the North Carolina Botanical Garden is covered with a magnificent ninety-year-old pine forest where most of the ground was beautiful but bleak in winter. Christmas ferns had begun to come back into it, and now the addition of big carpets of fifty to a hundred of them has livened it up. They were brought from the construction site of a new street, a rescue operation which brightens the woods in winter.

Ferns, by the sheer beauty and delicacy of their fronds, make the most elegant backgrounds and companions for wild flowers, especially the smaller ones. In winter, they contrast with the coarser foliage of other evergreens, each setting off the form of the other.

At this time of the year, the six-inch fronds of ebony spleenwort (*Asplenium platyneuron*) that have grown up amongst a patch of my tiny cyclamens create something unreal for delicate beauty. I simply have to stand and drink it in. In a few more weeks, the ivy-like leaves will arise from the cyclamen corms, and the flowers will be smothered out by frost time. Then the long fertile spleenwort fronds will disappear, leaving only their tiny evergreen fronds down among the cyclamen leaves for the winter show.

The Christmas fern, ebony spleenwort, the spinulose shield-fern (*Dryopteris spinulosa*), and the common polypody (*Polypodium vulgare*) will all live on acid to basic soil. The walking fern (*Adiantum camptosorus*) and the tiny maidenhair spleenwort (*A. trichomanes*) like lime and will not last long without it. Plaster from old walls is just what they like in their soil.

Start with a few ferns and learn about them. The lady in the late Helen Hokinson's cartoon was wrong when she said to the florist who offered her a fern, "Oh, no! They don't do anything!"

october tasks

Late October is the time to feed red spider lilies. Before the tree leaves fall, make the ground white with bone meal over the bulbs. A lot of them in old plantings will be right on the surface, but the bone meal will not damage them at all. Then a good feeding of complete fertilizer, such as 8-8-8, will nourish the bulbs and make a good set of leaves that will build up bulbs for next year. If you wait till the leaves have fallen, a lot of the bone meal and fertilizer will be absorbed by them, and the bulbs will have to wait a year to get the benefit of it.

Creeping phloxes can be divided now. The moss pink types and blue phloxes will make nice big clumps by spring, if they are taken up and divided and reset in good soil with some fertilizer before cold weather sets in. Our winters are so open that perennials of all kinds really do a lot of growing in all but the very bitterest weather.

All of the spreading spring perennials like Shasta daisies will benefit from lifting and dividing. September dividing is perhaps best, but October is acceptable. A little mulch over the newly transplanted perennials will give good protection and encourage growth of roots.

If you did not sow any winter annuals in September, order your seed now for a November planting. Chinese forget-me-nots, Iceland poppies, California poppies, and other "winter annuals" can be sown where they are to grow. They will probably not show up till warm days in February, but then they will grow off very fast. Pine needles are the cover, par excellence, for winter-sown annuals. You can raise a big crop of things like larkspur in a warm spot or in a cold frame from winter-sown seed. When the right time comes along, they will germinate and make deep roots even if not much growth shows up on top.

Some southern gardeners wait till November to plant sweet peas. In the coastal plains from Norfolk to Mexico, this is an excellent practice. (Up in the hills, it's pretty risky. Late winter is better.) Sow the seeds in well-prepared trenches of rich soil a little below the surface and bring the soil to the vines as they grow to get the maximum set of roots on them. Twigs and branches from shrubs and trees can be set in place before the sweet peas come up. These will not only provide the support needed in spring, but plastic can be fixed to the twigs to make a little greenhouse over the plants. Underneath this protection, the vines will grow apace, once they have got started, and produce a fine early crop of flowers. Well-established sweet peas will bloom on and on into the hot weather.

camellia companions

Over a hundred years ago, southern gardeners began planting camellias in their shady woodlands. Even where these beautiful shrubs were set out in the open in yards and gardens, trees eventually reached out over many of them and shaded them, so many of the finest camellias have been growing in part shade for years. Since camellias are native to the forests of China, they have thriven in our southern woodlands.

A great many of our camellia gardens or woodland areas where we grow them are more or less bare when the camellias are not in flower. This need not be so, however, because there are numerous shade-loving or shade-tolerant plants which will brighten up the woods.

Daylily fans soon found that hemerocallises of all kinds would flower in part shade. With the removal of low limbs from trees and the thinning out of the forest, just the right light is brought into woodlands to show off the flowers of shade lovers to the best advantage. The hot sun of our climate makes the partly shaded woodland one of the most pleasant places to enjoy flowers.

The shade-loving hydrangeas can be planted in conjunction with daylilies to good effect. The blue hortensias and the flat-topped "lace-cap" hydrangeas bloom with daylilies and provide a marvelous color scheme. Woodlands seem to provide the slight winter protection which

"I have seen all those cyclamens . . . and the glowing yellow host of
Sternbergia lutea.*"—Elizabeth Lawrence*

hydrangeas need to escape injury when the South has a real boreal winter.

At this time of the year when the red spider lilies have been in bloom, we should be reminded of how they will thrive in light woodland. Here and there, gardeners are beginning to plant the golden yellow sternbergias (*Sternbergia lutea*), now available from bulb dealers. They were quite a show at Williamsburg several weeks ago.

In half shade, the little common trumpet daffodil (*Narcissus pseudonarcissus*) will thrive and bloom at just the time in the spring when the camellias are playing out. This old tried-and-true daffodil can be interplanted with the sternbergias and the spider lilies to give fall and spring flowers. The spider lilies and sternbergias provide a handsome winter ground cover of foliage, and all three will go dormant just at the end of spring.

To extend the blooming period in these areas, plant also the big pink spider lily (*Lycoris squamigera*) to flower after midsummer. This big lycoris likes the same growing conditions as all the other bulbs, and all of them may be left without dividing for as long as ten years if the soil is prepared before they are planted. No bulbs should ever be planted in poor sand or clay because nothing can survive without good soil at least eight inches deep, good preparation, plus both bone meal and a complete fertilizer. After the bulbs have been planted, they can be top-fed in early November with a complete fertilizer one year and superphosphate the next.

fall and winter crocuses

Now is the time to plant fall and winter crocuses. Bulb catalogues and seed stores are offering them—more and more species and varieties each year—as American gardeners discover these tough little bulbs that bloom in spite of the winter cold.

The commonest autumn crocus is about out of bloom now. It is that beautiful little pink flower with the white throat that erupts into bloom in September. This one is *Crocus zonatus*, the best known of all.

About the time of the first frost, several forms of *C. speciosus* come into bloom. These little bulbs have been in my old garden for twenty years or more. I can always find them in the weeds when I go back there. It is native to eastern Europe, around the Black Sea to the

Caucasus and down into Iran. The flowers are borne on long white tubes that push them up amongst the fallen leaves in October and November. There are several named varieties that are delightful. 'Artabir', 'Cassiope', and 'Pollux' are selections from the wild form that were chosen and propagated by Messrs. van Tubergen in Holland. The variety 'Aitchisonii' has very large flowers that are spectacular for November flowers.

While it does not seem to stay more than a few years in my gardens, the famous saffron crocus (*C. sativus*) from whose stamens we get the saffron used in cooking and as a dyestuff, is certainly worth buying for your garden. Perhaps my soil is deficient in the lime it needs. Blooming at the same time is a real treasure, *C. longiflorus*. As the winter comes on, the long tubes emerge to greet the cold days and open their pink lilac, sweet-smelling flowers. This one was always a favorite of Mr. Bowles. Any flower which defies winter and gives off such a delightful odor in November would win a gardener's heart.

If you will search them out and plant them now, you can have some of the true winter-flowering crocuses. The first to flower for me, and one of the showiest, is *C. ancyrencis* which, like the September flowering *zonatus*, erupts into numerous little golden yellow flowers in January, right in the snow. How can such a tiny corm hold so many buds!

Next come the named varieties of *C chrysanthus*, which Mr. Bowles championed. He selected a number of beautiful variations and gave them the names of birds. 'Snow Bunting' is one of these, and the Dutch have introduced numerous other varieties. The crocuses come in many colors and shades from lavender to white and several combinations of purple and yellow.

I frequently remind gardeners to plant crocuses from four to six inches deep, but remember that there must be another four to six inches of good soil and a little steamed bone meal underneath the corms. Deep planting seems to give better protection from mice than a shallow planting.

daffodils for mass planting

Some kinds of daffodils seem to be permanent in southern gardens, while others last a few years and play out. Even in good soil, they just do not seem to want to stay with us. We know that the trumpets do not like the South much below middle Georgia, Alabama, Mississippi, and Louisiana. This is probably because the ground temperature in the Lower South is too high for them and the rainfall in summer more than they can tolerate.

The common little trumpet daffodils are certainly at home in the Upper South, however. They come from France and Spain on both sides of the Pyrenees where conditions are similar to those of our hill country.

Some of the big trumpets, descended from the Spanish and French wild species, make glorious masses in our gardens in spring. Old 'King Alfred' is a favorite all yellow. It got a First Class certificate from the Royal Horticultural Society in London in 1899. 'Emperor' (1890), 'Van Waveren's Giant' (1900), and 'Unsurpassable' (1929) have long since proven their worth. Among the well-behaved older white trumpets are 'Beersheba' (1925) and 'Mount Hood' (1938). 'Empress' (1890) is a good, old two-toned yellow trumpet likely to be found in all old gardens today because of its lasting qualities.

Daffodil fanciers may look down on these old kinds, but they are the proven, older varieties that have stayed with us. They are also the most likely ones to be found in stores at bottom prices. They cost so little that gardeners can indulge themselves with big beds of daffodils in the spring. A few daffodils are beautiful, but a lot are thrilling!

When it comes to the early kinds, the famous two-toned 'Fortune', a "large-cupped" flower, is always exciting, even if late frosts do sometimes topple the flowers over by freezing the stem right at the ground. This bulb has been gathering honors since 1923. In the *Classified List of Daffodil Names* of the Royal Horticultural Society, it is listed with no less than seven English and Dutch awards. Everybody knows that 'February Gold' (1923) does not bloom in February (maybe it does in the Deep South), but it is a tough old daffodil that blooms well.

The lovely white, or cream, twin-flowered 'Thalia' of van Waveren (1916) stayed high in price for years—perhaps because it was so very popular. It is of special value not only for its breathtaking beauty in a mass planting but also because it flowers just before, and overlapping with, the dogwoods. In my old garden, the mass of white seemed to leap from the ground to the trees in three days. This one likes Deep South gardens, too.

Space is too limited for more old "good-doers," but 'Carbineer' (1927) a "large-cupped Narcissus with red cup" always stays with us when many other kinds have begun to need digging and feeding. Its color holds up in spring rains and early hail storms.

the ghost house of natchez

The maintenance and restoration of the fine old houses and mansions built when cotton was king on the high bluffs at Natchez and up and down the Mississippi have required so much money that the landscapes and some of the old gardens down there have disappeared. Most people who have visited Natchez can never forget the fantastic unfinished Moorish-Byzantine mansion called Longwood. It is sometimes called the ghost house and was also called Nutt's Folly after Dr. Haller Nutt, the original owner. Surely no house in the South is more interesting or has a more fascinating history. The grounds and gardens at Longwood were both elaborate and extensive. After I gave a lecture to the Pilgrimage Garden Club there, we met in conference concerning the restoration of these once fabulous gardens.

It is said that the mistress of Longwood, the beautiful red-headed Julia Augusta Williams Nutt, used to go a mile through her rose gardens gathering flowers. The portraits of her and of her husband Dr. Haller Nutt reveal two sensitive and intelligent people. In her portrait, Julia is holding a rose.

Longwood Villa was barely started when "the war" broke out in April, 1861. News of firing on Fort Sumter alarmed the workmen, and they fled north on the next packet boats. Ninety years later, Harnett Kane wrote that he visited the still unfinished 100-foot-high mansion. He had gone around the basement of the old structure with one of the descendants of the Nutt family, and they found the work clothes of one of the painters who fled on that April day in 1861 still hanging from a chair near a partly painted wall!

Restoration of the gardens at Longwood will be a great gift to the South. The period just before the Civil War was one of great opulence—certainly so around the wealthy Mississippi and Louisiana cotton plantations where the owners were vying with each other in showing off their great wealth. Furniture for the huge houses they built was imported from Europe, as anyone who has visited Natchez well knows.

This was the great era of tea roses and of many kinds of climbing roses. For the past thirty or forty years, a small group of "old roses nuts," as we have been called, has been collecting the old-fashioned varieties all over the South. Cleo Barnwell and others have been propagating them in Shreveport, and they are supplying plants for the tea rose garden at Briarwood.

Jo Evans and Cleo Barnwell and I have searched the old cemetery at Natchez for old roses. Don't miss this fascinating cemetery; it has the tombs of Spanish grandees as well as of famous French and American families.

Pomegranates, the hardy orange (*Citrus trifoliata*), "sweet syringa" (*Philadelphus coronaris*), and hydrangeas, were among the favorites of gardeners in the mid-1800s. There were no Kurume azaleas. Andrew Jackson had seen them at Mobile and tried to grow them at The Hermitage, but he probably killed them with cow manure! Many of the native plants like gransy grey-beard or fringe tree were greatly appreciated in this era. The restoration at Longwood will be very interesting.

new orleans' longue vue gardens

The old gardens that disappeared after 1861 at Longwood in Natchez were some of the most elaborate and interesting ever planted. But Longue Vue House in New Orleans certainly has one of the most beautiful and unusual of modern gardens. The gift of the late Mr. and Mrs. Edgar Stern, Longue Vue is open to the public.

Edith Stern went to Spain, and with the great care with which she always did everything, measured the famous fountains at the Alhambra and the Generalife. Her copies of these fountains are works of art, and Longue Vue is a garden not to be missed.

New Orleans is very excited about the coming centennial of the Great Cotton Exposition of 1884–85 which they will celebrate soon. In doing research on the historic restoration of these old gardens, I searched my library and found *Nouveau Jardinier de la Louisiane*, which gave instructions on planting and had lists of the best flowers and shrubs for the New Orleans area, some of which have changed greatly in a century. The zinnias they had in those days, for example, were not the monsters of today. There were simple forms of many of our garden flowers. Growing some of them in the New Orleans climate presented some problems. As luck would have it, I found another very appropriate title: *Guide to New Orleans, 1884–85,* a treasure that tells everything about everybody as well as about the great improvements that were taking place in the city in the way of parks and gardens. The old straight beds were giving way to the new curved style, and many, many new plants had by then been introduced. One plant that the South has regretted to see proliferating and clogging up the waterways of the Deep South is the water hyacinth. It has always been said that the water hyacinth was introduced at the great New Orleans exposition.

In 1941, I designed New Orleans' first city-wide flower show. Mrs. C. S. Williams—with the beautiful French name Delphine—had a house in Biltmore Forest, and I took the plans up there in the middle of the summer for the consideration of the committee. The show was staged in the "small section" of New Orleans' then new auditorium. Since New Orleans people are accustomed to stopping at nothing when they stage the annual Mardi Gras, I dared to ask for all sorts of things, even for one of those huge oil jars used to ornament their patios—and they produced it!

The roses in New Orleans in October and November, and the ginger lilies, are something a gardener can never forget, and I am sure they will be features of the next great exposition along with the "new" plants like *Camellia sasanqua* which I encouraged the New Orleans Gardening Society to plant in Audubon Park back in the thirties—of *this* century.

frost protection

The first few frosts need not take off all of your flowers. Many of our garden plants are highly resistant to frost and can have a longer life right into November if you are willing to take the trouble to cover them up on frosty nights. While it is not practical to cover up a whole garden, at least a few of the late chrysanthemums and big, healthy petunias can be protected for the gardener's pleasure a long time after the first frosts. Remember that snapdragons can stand a lot of cold, too, and you may be surprised at other plants in the garden that try to stand up to the low temperatures.

Here in the South, we are apt to have a frost or two followed by a balmy Indian summer for ten days to two weeks. It always seems a pity to me that we do not protect a few flowers during these little frosts and enjoy them during the fine autumn weather. Our grandmothers did not give up all their flowers with the coming of intermittent frosts. Front yards and small gardens in the country used to bloom with the stars and flowers of handmade quilts in early autumn. As soon as morning came, off came the quilts and out came the chrysanthemums and dahlias.

In colder parts of the world, plant covers called cloches are set over choice flowers at night. When I was stationed in Brussels during World War II, I used to walk through the Jardin Botanique in the early morning, and I enjoyed looking down onto beds of early flowering megaseas all covered up with mats. By noon, the mats were off and the flowers in full bloom. We can also learn a great deal from the Japanese about covering plants up. Their gardens are beautiful in winter with handsomely contrived straw plant covers almost as beautiful as flowers.

Just before the killing frosts some of your plants can be potted up and brought inside. Late chrysanthemums can finish their blooming in the house. Petunias are great for this; they will flower in a pot in a sunny window. When they have finished, cut them back and watch them start all over again. Petunias are really perennials that will flower over and over. During mild winters here in the South petunias live over winter at the foot of a sunny wall—even in cold sections.

Many gardeners pick pansies all winter from a bed covered with plastic. They are some of the very best coolhouse plants for bloom during the winter months. The bright, cheery blossoms are a delight to everybody. Plant some now in pots and bring them in. They want only sunshine and a fairly cool house. In hot houses, they will bloom themselves out shortly and perish.

Dig a few snapdragons and bring them in. Old plants can be cut back and will come out immediately and begin to flower in a few weeks in a window. We never seem to smell them in the garden, but in the house, you will enjoy their peculiar, sweet fragrance.

perpetual-flowering roses

Our perpetual-flowering modern roses have come to us through some very noble ancestors. Like most wild plants, the wild roses of the world do not flower but once a year. A kindly Nature, however, does remarkable things, and She created for us gardeners, way back in the centuries before Christ, a rose, a very few varieties of which had the habit of blooming a second time after their spring or early summer flowering. From these miraculous plants, we have today our continuous-flowering modern roses.

The late Dr. C. C. Hurst, in his history of our garden roses in the *Journal of the Royal Horticultural Society*, tells us that the old autumn damask roses are very ancient. They were used on the island of Samos, in the cult of Aphrodite (Venus), as early as the tenth century B.C., because of their habit of flowering twice a year. These reblooming roses were prized for the production of flowers for the Greek and Roman feasts in which literally tons of roses were used. Rose nurseries were planted in Egypt to supply flowers for the Roman market in winter.

The reblooming roses that sprang up from the Samos roses were carried all around the Mediterranean and even down into Abyssinia. They picked up many names from the places where they were grown: Rose of Alexandria, the Paestum Rose, the Rose of Damascus. When the Arabs invaded Spain, the roses they took with them were these reblooming plants.

Dr. Hurst tells us that a beautiful Chinese rose was introduced into Italy by the sixteenth century. One was recorded in bloom in Italy in November of 1678, so it seems strange that these oriental remontant, i.e., reblooming, roses did not reach England until the nineteenth century.

With two remontant roses in the gardens of the world, it is not surprising that they finally met and mated, but the reputed place for the romance is strange indeed: the tiny little French island of Bourbon in the Indian Ocean! There is much speculation about whether or not this was the first time the two species had met, but the beautiful progeny of this union soon had the French nurserymen agog and producing new varieties that brought them a lot of money.

Gardeners of today still grow one of the Bourbon roses: 'Souvenir de la Malmaison'. Here in the South, old gardens have some handsome specimens of this beauty. Rose lovers know that Malmaison, the Empress Josephine's palace, once had the finest collection of roses in the world, and it was as her court painter that Redouté painted his roses. Even during the wars with England, roses were allowed through the lines to Josephine's garden from everywhere.

The Bourbon roses, with their genes for reblooming, soon gave rise to the hybrid perpetuals. They, in turn, were the parents of the modern tea rose, and since their creation, the genes of all sorts of roses have combined to give us the magnificent roses of today.

spring and summer perennials

It's time to set out perennial plants. During the long sunshiny days of autumn and early winter, the little plants will grow apace and bloom lustily next spring and summer. (Fall-flowering perennials are best divided and replanted in spring.)

After a long lull, the interest in perennials is reviving. The dazzling azaleas and the camellias, both *japonica* and *sasanqua*, stole the show for a long time, but gardeners are beginning to realize that the many easily grown perennials provide beautiful effects in the landscape as well as in the borders. Shrubs do not provide much in the way of cut flowers. People got the idea that shrubs needed little attention, but they know better now, and they are finding that perennials do not require much more effort.

Probably the first thing one should take into account in selecting perennials is their ultimate shape and height and the space they will need when fully grown. Some kinds will remain in the garden almost permanently. The big perennials like peonies need a lot of space and can be treated like shrubs.

Some of the spike types of perennials and biennials are foxgloves, hollyhocks, the salvias, some mallows, goldenrod, sidalcea, mulleins, veronicas, blazing or gayfeathers (*Liatris*), lupins, physostegias, delphiniums (if you can grow them), the bugbanes or snakeroot (*Cimicifuga*), astilbes, and monkshood (*Aconitum*). English gardeners like to grow our yuccas in the backs of their groups. The big red-hot pokers *(Kniphofia)* are very effective as accents anywhere.

There are a great many perennials of the clump type like the phloxes, achilleas, asters, Shasta daisies, Chinese delphinium (one you can keep going even in southern gardens), geums, baby's breath, irises, *Sedum spectabile*, and spiderworts. The veronicas and lythrum provide both clumps and spikes.

Then there are the mass types like some phloxes and monardas. These need lifting and dividing every few years when they have spent their soil's fertility. There are many fine, low masses for the front of borders. The creeping veronicas, plumbago (now *Ceratostigma*), perennial candytuft, creeping phloxes, thyme, pinks, sedums, and a number of "rock-garden" creepers. One of the best of these is the little cypress spurge (*Euphorbia cyparissias*) that was left over from the rock-garden craze back in the thirties. Light green, feathery foliage and light yellow heads of flowers in spring make it an excellent permanent plant.

When all these architectural types are put together carefully, they make real works of art, as anyone who has ever seen an English border can tell you. The English have gone back to perennials, if they can be considered ever to have left them. Alan Bloom's garden at his nursery in Essex is a real perennials dream, and his book *Hardy Perennials for the Garden* will inspire you. Another beautiful and informative book is Anthony Huxley's *Garden Perennials and Water Plants.*

the long color season

The long season of colored leaves really began back in July and August when a few cool nights followed some sizzling days. It was then that a few young sourwoods began to redden up. On the black gums, the effect of this temperature change showed up on a branch here and there; a sign that summer was on the way out. The tulip trees had known this all along. They had begun to show some golden leaves for several weeks before that.

As October approached, all of a sudden the dogwoods began to lose their summer green for a pale yellow green that made them stand out in distinct masses before the dark woods. Redbuds went gradually into pale, bright yellows, and the big, heart-shaped leaves began floating down. When the night temperature went down to the forties and the day up to eighty, that did it; the color season was on. Red maples and sweet gums began at their tips. In three days they were colored all over. The shiny-leaved black gums and the dogwoods caught fire against the blue skies brought in with cold air from the northwest.

The weathermen say these early cold spells which we have seen coming to the South for the past few years are the result of a shift of one of the jet streams very high above the United States and Canada. They claim that this shift is probably also responsible for the change in the paths of hurricanes, farther east. After one of those hurricanes went to the Azores, I was pleased to hear of a big rain in drought-stricken England.

As November approaches, the color season that began in the southern mountains has come to us in the hills. Red maples seem to specialize in reds and oranges. Southern sugar maples turn mostly to yellows. (If you want to be sure of the magnificent colors in sugar maples every year, it is best to get some trees from the northern nurseries.) Black gums take on perhaps the deepest reds, except for those of a few sweet gums. Sweet gums are the multicolored specialists, from deep black violet to light pinks, oranges, and rose. Some of them turn almost blue. This is the tree that Europeans covet!

Sweet gums (*Liquidambar styraciflua*) are not related to the tupelos and black gums (*Nyssa sylvatica*). They were called sweet gums because of the gum that oozes from their trunks when they are wounded. To the world of wooden ships—the old countries seeking spices for their salted meats—the products of the New World were wonderful indeed.

After all the other leaves have fallen in November, the scarlet oak will bring on its fiery color. Up in the Blue Ridges, the northern red oak will put on unbelievable burgundy reds, but only a few tree lovers ever see this spectacle which comes after the big show. In the sandhills, the turkey and blackjack oaks are a feast of colors against the pines long after frosts have come.

november

early spring bulbs

Now is the time to plan for that wonderful period in southern gardens: late winter and very early spring. When the sunshine of late winter days and the occasional warm rains come, the earliest flowering bulbs begin to bloom. Cool days and cold nights are just what hyacinths, the early daffodils, and some of the spectacular new tulips delight in. Most flowers bloom for a period of about ten days in our gardens, but these early bulbs will last for two weeks or even longer, unless rains spoil them. They are probably the most worthwhile flowers of the year. They will open in spite of frosty temperatures and stand up to the cold amazingly. In fact, you will probably be wearing an overcoat to go out and see them. Be sure to locate one bed where you can look at it from the window.

We are blessed in the South with that tough, frost-hardy, little yellow trumpet daffodil (*Narcissus pseudonarcissus*) from southern France and the rugged, cold Pyrenees of northern Spain. It has spread and spread until there are masses of it all over the southern states. Everybody delights in its early gold, and everybody passes it on to new gardeners. For your early spring show, begin with this old bulb.

Hyacinths of all kinds are a joy for this cold time when crocuses have usually begun to fade with the rains. They resist the cold, and along with the earliest daffodils, last longer in a garden than almost anything one can plant. In a good, well-drained situation they will go on for years. Wet feet they will not tolerate; they will rot and disappear. The tiny chionodoxas are, in effect, just little hyacinths and need the same conditions. They will multiply from seed when they are happy and cover the ground around them with seedlings. For some unexplainable reason, we have never planted them very much in the South. Anything as delicate and tough that is blue is a desirable bulb for us.

Then brighten your treasure house with some of the early single and double tulips. The old Darwin hybrid 'Kaiserkroon', gold and red, is still a good one, and the yellows, whites, and pinks in these early kinds are popular, but some wonderful new tulips have been added to these earliest ones.

The gardening world was amazed at the brilliant, big tulip called 'Red Emperor' (*Tulipa fosteriana*) when it came out some years ago. One can hardly believe that anything that tall and gaudy could possibly bloom in such cool weather. Its tall stems need to be tied to an invisible wire if it is grown where winds will blow it down. This tulip springs from a wild species around Samarcand and Bokhara.

From the area of those red, black, and white rugs of Turkestan, two other brilliant, wild tulips came into cultivation back in the nineteenth century, *T. kaufmanniana* and *T. greigii*. From them have come the water-lily tulips and the peacock tulips, respectively. The striped-leaved peacock varieties have foliage that would be beautiful enough to justify their place in the garden even if they never had a flower. They are cold hardy and sturdy. Some are low and some fairly tall. The flowers are usually yellow, in many shades, bordered with other colors, and they stand there for days and days in the cool weather as if they were china figurines.

The water-lily group has big flowers which open up wide in the sun and they do indeed look like fantastic water lilies. Both of these new groups of tulips thrive here in the South. They like our hot summers better than they do the wet English climate where they have to be lifted and dried every year. You will find all these new tulips as named cultivars in stores and catalogues.

the little bulbs

There are many sorts of little bulbs which gardeners in the South do not seem to grow. Beginning in December and January, the winter crocuses begin to flower whenever the temperature rises above freezing. They are startling, to say the least. The yellow crocus 'E. A. Bowles' is perhaps the best known cultivar.

In January and February, the little hoop-petticoat daffodils bloom on sunny days. Some of the choicest ones are white and bloom in November and December. You will have to look for the full name *Narcissus bulbocodium citrinus* to get the lemon yellow ones. The bulbs are unbelievably tiny. The variety *conspicuus* does not bloom until spring and is an orange yellow.

From Spain comes the astonishing, tiny trumpet daffodil, *N. asturiensis.* It blows its tiny trumpet in my woods in January or February— sometimes in the snow—and it is always insulted if I do not come down immediately and admire it. Asturia is one of the hottest parts of Spain, so this tiny piece of floral jewelry wants a warm spot in the winter garden. Be sure to plant five of these little bulbs in a pot and sink the pot in the ground near the spot where you plant the others. Any time after Christmas, you can bring the pot into the house and have a miniature trumpet fanfare on your windowsill.

Later on in the spring, there are some other small daffodils from Spain and Portugal that like southern gardens. One of these is the rush-leaved daffodil, *N. juncifolius.* The flowers are all of three-fourths of an inch across with a tiny cup in the middle. This one seeds itself in the path in my old garden. Two more of these little things are *N. rupicola* and *N. scaberulus,* and they seem to come easily from seed, too.

In the Tazetta group of narcissi, there is a beautiful little flower that is a cut-down version of a paper-white, except that it has a tiny golden cup. Although the bulbs are offered frequently in catalogues, and I buy them from time to time, this one (*N. canaliculatus*) will not bloom up in the hill country but once. It survives the winters but refuses ever to flower again! It probably longs for the warmer winter of the coastal plain.

For a charming miniature in early spring, one cannot do better than *Chionodoxa luciliae.* This bulb seems to be permanent in all of my old gardens. Of course, the tiny *Hyacinthus amethystinus* and *H. azureus* are miniature hyacinths. Then, for real Prussian blue in late winter, *Scilla sibirica* is the bulb. Patches of these scillas close to a path will cheer you on cold days—and amaze you.

a garden visit

A visit to Elizabeth Lawrence's garden is always delightful and stimulating. I found her waiting at the door last week, and we went right into the garden. What a treasure house of fine plants! Even as far north as Charlotte, North Carolina, Elizabeth had a loquat (*Eriobotrya japonica*) in bloom. Way up in the top of her arbutus tree, the California Madrone (*Arbutus menziesii*), were a few blossoms, too. Like many tender trees and shrubs, the arbutus can stand the low temperatures if it can get through enough winters to develop some good-size stems. Horticulturists say, "if you can get some wood on it." Even crape myrtles have been grown in Harrisburg, Pennsylvania, when they were taken there with some old wood on them.

Gardeners always love to give each other plants: "You mean you don't have the fine-leaved feather ivy?—it came from South Carolina." So we went and found a digging fork, pruners, trowel, and deep hand fork and proceeded to dig small pieces of all her fancy ivies.

In the shaded back garden, I admired a huge patch of the supposedly tender *Iris japonica* and exclaimed over what a handsome ground cover it made. "Oh you gave it to me years ago when I first saw your winter irises in bloom," she said. This little evergreen plant looks somewhat like the roof iris of Japan, *I. tectorum*. It is a wonderful plant for Deep South gardeners. Although the foliage is quite evergreen, a very cold winter seems to prevent it from forming bloom buds, or perhaps the low temperatures freeze the flower buds, so that it does not bloom every year. Here this iris, tender as it is, was growing under the canopy of some rare magnolias. As with many mature gardens, the back part of Elizabeth's had grown up into handsome trees which had shaded out many of the shrubs but at the same time provided ideal protection for tender plants.

Elizabeth has a large specimen of the rare *Camellia saluenensis*. The flowers are single and not very big, but they resist the cold and flower all winter, beginning toward the end of November. The early blooming 'Donation', 'Apple Blossoms', 'J. C. Williams', and 'Mary Christian' are all derived from this cold-hardy Chinese species.

I went around to her iron gateway to see her evergreen *Clematis armandii*. After the leaves have fallen from the trees in autumn, it is amazing to see evergreen clematis foliage. Another clematis (*C. calycina*) with little bells the size of your finger was in full bloom on the house up too high to examine.

Not many people have a plant of the strange butcher's broom (*Ruscus aculeatus*), and not many gardeners have ever seen red berries on a butcher's broom. But many of us have had seeds of Elizabeth's specimen, which is sticking full of the red fruits every fall.

In spite of warm, muggy weather, her fall-blooming cherry (*Prunus subhirtella* 'Autumnalis') was not in flower. She insisted on sharing with me a piece of rare silene, given to her by Fred Galle of Callaway Gardens at Pine Mountain, Georgia. The generous habit of sharing plants is one of the best ways to keep fine plants going for future gardeners.

Elizabeth Lawrence's book, *A Southern Garden*, is still one of the most charmingly written and informative books on southern gardening. It was written when she lived in Raleigh, North Carolina. When it went out of print, I urged the University of North Carolina Press at Chapel Hill to reprint it. This printed edition, with some new material about her Charlotte garden, is still available.

camellia sasanqua

Intermittent cold snaps and frosts do not destroy the effect of *Camellia sasanqua* in November and December. These beautiful, big shrubs produce so many buds that when one set of flowers is damaged or destroyed by the cold, more buds open up and keep the show going. Late varieties are still blooming under the leaves after Christmas. The larger the shrub gets, the more protection it offers the flowers that open back inside the bush.

We southern gardeners are missing something in not training the late-flowering varieties of *sasanqua* on walls for a December show. These camellias have an abundance of branches that are easily trained on a trellis or right onto a wall. In England, where gardeners grow many tender things in this way, they are a great show in the collections of camellia fans in winter. One annual pruning, right after flowering, seems to hold back the growth sufficiently to keep them from running away.

They will take more sun than *Camellia japonica* usually likes. This allows for their being used in hedges that stand in both sun and shade. While shearing or clipping can be done, the big, loose *sasanqua* hedge that is not trimmed or pruned is the most beautiful of all. It is this loose effect of the branches and foliage that makes them so appealing.

They just naturally like our southern climate. The hot summers and occasional droughts probably ripen their wood and make them hardy to cold. One of the most beautiful gardens in all of Italy was planted by a Scotsman, Neil McEacharn, on Lago Maggiore. Way up there in north ern Italy, the climate is much like that of parts of our southern states: high temperature at times in summer, lots of rain, and sudden temperature drops in fall and winter—also fierce droughts at times. In spite of all this, *sasanqua* grows and thrives and is a feature of this garden at Villa Taranto. In 1953, McEacharn wrote, *"Camellia sasanqua* is a great feature in our collection of camellias, providing a mass of bloom from October till April. It is a most satisfactory shrub, as neither cold nor rain nor frost hinder its delicate flowers, and I have even seen big plants covered with flowers when the gound was white with snow." Doesn't all this sound like our southern climate?

Good plantsmen try out all kinds of plants from all over the world and find out what will grow well in any climate. The late Mr. K. Sawada was just such a man here in the South. He grew *sasanqua* varieties years ago in his nursery near Mobile and showed us how wonderful they were.

The habit they have of shedding their petals over the ground has not been popular with some gardeners, but surely the petal-covered ground underneath these beauties is one of their charms! In the cool fall weather, the petals stay in good condition for several days.

The beautiful, snow white 'Mine-no-yuki' is just finishing its bloom now. This dazzling white variety can nearly always be counted upon for Thanksgiving. It has a great use in the landscape where you want a spreading *sasanqua* instead of an upright one. Old specimens, nevertheless, build up slowly until they reach the second stories of houses. The most dramatic setting of a 'Mine-no-yuki' with which I am acquainted is at the corner of a house with an outside stairway beside the shrub. One can ascend the stairs accompanied all the way to the top by this "snow-on-the-mountain" as some gardeners call it.

apples

Nothing adds a more comfortable feeling to a garden than an old apple tree. If you have one, prune it and love it and nurture it—even if it is falling down. As the old lady and the old man sang in their duet in *The Boy Friend,* "A ruin can be beautiful."

Apples have been favorite fruits of Europeans since back before Roman times. They were grown solely for the making of cider for several centuries before the English and French began to select seedlings for eating and cooking.

Up until thirty or forty years ago, there were all sorts of delicious cooking and eating apples. Beginning in the summer, there were 'Red June', 'Yellow Transparent', 'Summer Rose', 'Red Astrachan', and many more that made the most delicious applesauce. When I was a boy living in the neighborhood of my uncle's nursery, we always had applesauce on the table. It was as much a staple as grits; applesauce makes everything else on the table taste better.

When fall came, 'Grimes Golden' was something to look forward to, with its slightly banana-like flavor. Some old orchards in the mountains still have a few trees of this wonderful apple, but it was not big, and Stark's 'Golden Delicious' has superseded it. If you ever eat a 'Grimes Golden', you will realize that 'Golden Delicious' is only faintly reminiscent of it. 'Winesap' and 'Virginia Beauty' and 'York Imperial'—these were popular southern apples. To say these names makes one's mouth water! They always ripened way in the winter and hung on the trees till cold weather. Then you had to look for them down among the leaves. They were firm but juicy. In the North, they grew 'Baldwin' and 'Jonathan' and 'Northern Spy'.

The apples of today must be as hard as baseballs in order to lend themselves well to shipping across the country. This requirement has eliminated most of the really delicious apples. What we get in the stores are, to an apple lover, tasteless—except for one. In 'Stayman Winesap' we have a wonderful apple that can be shipped because it is very firm up until it ripens. Look for these beautiful, juicy apples in the store and plant this variety in your garden—or a good summer apple like 'Yellow Transparent'. This one has not disappeared from the nurseries. The apples will cook into sauce almost by the time they come to a boil—and such applesauce!

pansies

Pansies got their name from the French word *pensée* ("thought"). Ophelia says in Shakespeare's *Hamlet*, "There is pansies, that's for thoughts." In the language of the flowers, this must have meant amorous or, at least, sentimental thoughts.

Pansies, so beloved of gardeners today, were developed from one or more wild violets. Their chief ancestor was a European violet called Heartsease (Ophelia's pansy). It is no wonder, then, that these flowers have been associated with sentiment. Pansies, violets, violas, and Johnny-jump-ups all belong to the genus *Viola*.

Since violets have been such popular garden flowers, in fact, next in popularity to the rose, it seems strange they were not developed until the beginning of the last century. From the earliest European history, poets, painters, and writers have celebrated the beauty of the violet. Persians listed violets in their floras. The Arabs grew them in their gardens in Spain, and during the Renaissance, the monks grew them in monastery gardens. Edward A. Bunyard, an authority on old roses, claimed that it was really Napoleon who caused the "violet furor" in France because, when he left for Elba, he said, "I shall be back with the violets in spring."

Our modern pansies were developed in England around 1810 by T. Thomson, gardener to Lord Gambier at Iver in Buckinghamshire. By 1825 there were some 400 named varieties! In France and Belgium, still more named varieties appeared and were called Fancy Pansies. Our Exhibition pansies came from these beauties.

Their ability to stand up to the cold winter weather has led to their great popularity in the South. The way they take the extreme cold of a bad winter is unbelievable. Only those that are planted very late or set out in poor soil or in extremely exposed places seem to care how cold it gets. The least little bit of protection is very effective in keeping them growing right through the cold weather. A small topdressing of cow manure makes them prosper. If you want flowers for the house in December and January, pot a few and bring them in and set them on a cool windowsill. In a cold frame outside, they will bloom lustily. Keep the flowers picked to keep them from throwing their strength into seeds.

There are numerous strains of pansies listed in seed catalogues. Many people get their pansy plants from church organizations by ordering them in September for November delivery. This has become an institution that may have as much to do with pansy popularity as Napoleon did with the violets of his day.

berries in the woods

After the leaves are down, all the berried jewels of the southern woods reveal themselves. The huge masses of shiny red berries are apt to be the fruits of one of the nonevergreen hollies. The commonest one likes the sunlight of the edges of fields and puts on a big show, discernable even at great distances, along roads and fencerows. This one is *Ilex decidua*. The berries range in color from bright red to striking orange reds. I have seen some orange ones that made me want to jump off the train as I traveled on lecture trips over the South—especially in Mississippi, Louisiana, and East Texas.

Highways are beautified by our sumacs. These running shrubs of the genus *Rhus* are so persistent that they take over bare banks for themselves. Bittersweet (*Celastrus scandens*) is a vine that does the same thing. Wherever bittersweet has been cultivated in yards and gardens, you can be sure that it will have gone off by itself and taken over its own world. The berries are so beloved by everybody that usually no one lifts a finger to remove the vines until they get completely out of hand, like wisteria.

One of our most beautiful natives, a big shrub or small tree, is sparkleberry (*Vaccinium arboreum*), in effect a huge, dry-berried huckleberry. The fine foliage, extremely shiny berries, and brown trunk of this exquisite shrub are only some of its virtues; the tiny bells that cover its branches in spring or early summer are a breathtaking sight. Some specimens that I know in old cemeteries in the South would make the most sophisticated English or Japanese plant lovers gasp. In fact, my slides of it do just that to them.

The different names that people have given to native plants over the southern states are fascinating. Caroline Dormon, who shared my love of sparkleberry, called it winter huckleberry. Her drawing of a twig of it with a bird eating the shiny little black berries is charming. The tiny leaves of sparkleberry stay green until the real cold snaps come along. Then the foliage begins to turn red, but remains on the bush until, by January, they are ablaze, and it is only in February that the leaves finally drop and reveal the twisted trunks.

In her book *Natives Preferred*, Caroline says that she never has seen *V. arboreum* in a catalogue. Since this tree-shrub grows in dryish places, it will tolerate dry places in yards and gardens but does not seem to demand such a site. Caroline warns that only little tiny ones are easy to transplant and that they like acid soil like the azaleas. They can be seen in some azalea gardens in the South.

If you do not already own Caroline Dormon's books: *Flowers Native to the Deep South* and *Natives Preferred*, and Elizabeth Lawrence's

Gardens in Winter, your bookstore will get them for you from Claitor's Book Store, P.O. Box 239, Baton Rouge, Louisiana 70821.

plant for the birds

Every acre that is taken from our woods and turned into commercial property or used for residences cuts down on the available wild food for our birds. It really behooves gardeners to plant food for them and keep their population from diminishing.

Fortunately, many of our ornamental trees and shrubs are good providers. Every pyracantha is inhabited by a mockingbird. On cold mornings, you can see him perched atop his bush, looking lovingly at the splendid larder of bright berries which will see him through the winter. Yaupons are equally attractive to them. I was once on a visit to Mrs. William Du Pont at Jacksonville, Florida, and as we walked around her formal garden, we were attacked by a mocker as we passed each big yaupon.

All of the viburnums and the photinias and hollies provide bird food. Photinias and *Viburnum rhytidophyllum* take some time to get big enough to produce much of a crop, but when they are mature, they set a feast. Some hollies seem to ripen slowly through the winter. The berries may not be touched until early March when cedar waxwings clean them up en route back to the North. The berries of other kinds of holly are eaten as early as Christmas.

In wet places, you can plant chokeberries (*Pyrus arbutifolia*) and black alder. The red chokeberries are the showier ones. If you plant a few bushes five feet apart, they will spread by underground suckers and make a brilliant patch of berries. The black alder is actually a holly (*Ilex verticillata*) that likes the edge of a stream. Berries of this ilex are some of the earliest to turn red in autumn.

The fruit-eating birds love crab apples of all kinds. These trees make splendid nesting places for the resident birds, who, in return, help to destroy fruit-tree pests. One has to watch for patches of scale around old bird nests, however. These tiny crawling insects apparently get on the feet of birds and are carried to nesting sites in summer, where they make a wax cover over themselves and infest the tree or shrub. After the leaves are off, a miscible oil spray will destroy the scale.

If you really want to enjoy birds in summer, plant just one Russian mulberry tree (*Morus alba tatarica*). Birds will come from far and near all during the several weeks when the mulberries are ripening.

I heard a white-throated sparrow's sweet autumn call three weeks ago. Juncos and purple finches are due any day now, and fox sparrows will soon be scratching like chickens amongst the leaves with the towhees, so get your sunflower seeds and baby-chick feed ready—and plenty of both for the winter.

southern oak trees

The southern states are a treasure house of different kinds of oak trees. White oak, red oak, black oak, scarlet oak, live oak, water oak, pin oak—these are the better-known species and the ones we grow as shade trees. There are, however, other handsome oaks that are hardly known to the public because we still do not appreciate our trees, and so it has not paid nurserymen to grow them for us.

Because of the fact that white oaks (*Quercus alba*) do no grow very fast, we have neglected to plant many of them. The faster-growing willow oaks (*Q. phellos*) and the so-called Darlington oak (*Q. laurifolia*) have been planted in quantity all over the southern states. In the coastal plains from Norfolk to Mexico, people have planted live oaks (*Q. virginiana*) and the smaller laurel oak (*Q. laurifolia*). Pin oaks (*Q. palustris*) have been available from some nurseries. They are good for moist land, and their weeping lower branches are unusually graceful.

The scarlet oak (*Q. coccinea*), the dazzling beauty that comes afire with color after all the other trees have shed their leaves, is scarcely available from southern nurseries. If you want one, you may have to transplant a seedling from the woods.

The cow oak, or swamp chestnut oak (*Q. michauxii*), and the rock chestnut oak (*Q. prinus*) are fine trees. In southern swamps or low places along streams, there are many fine specimens of the spreading cow oak, which resembles the white oak of the hills and mountains. On the tops of low mountains in the piedmont and on most of the real mountains, the rock chestnut oak, with leaves of the same shape as those of the cow oak grows in amongst the rocks and huge boulders. This slow-growing, hardy tree with its deeply furrowed bark stands up to the coldest winds of winter. The heavy wood resists forest fires so well that it was used for railroad ties in the areas where it was available, in spite of the great difficulty of cutting it. Acorns of this tree are some of the largest. This time of the year they are falling with a great thud.

Wherever the long-leaf pine grows—and where it used to grow—the little turkey oaks (*Q. laevis*) are ablaze right now. These little trees and the blackjack oaks (*Q. marilandica*) can grow on the worst kinds of sandy and poor clay soils. Wherever they have been left to grow in yards and gardens, they make beautiful specimen trees.

Two oaks with especially beautiful acorns are the mossycup, sometimes called bur oak (*Q. macrocarpa*), and the overcup oak (*Q. lyrata*). The bur-like cups that enclose the acorns of the bur oak do look decidedly mossy. They make splendid decorations, and so do the cups and acorns of the overcup, whose cups cover the acorns almost completely.

These are only some of the fine oak species growing here in the South. If we do not begin to cultivate them, we shall soon have to go to the botanical gardens and southern arboretums—or perhaps to England and Europe—to see our own native trees.

leaves galore

Leaves, leaves, leaves! The trees have brought in their rich harvest and spread it over the earth. Only a few years ago people dreaded November's leaf fall. Today, they are clamoring for leaves for their gardens and compost piles. Old sawdust piles and rotten slabs are being sought out for their riches, and cities are unable to supply vegetable gardeners with all the leaves they want. We have come to our senses.

As soon as they fall, the leaves begin to be broken down by the millions of tiny organisms that turn them into the humus that builds topsoil. In forests of the southern states where the land was never cultivated, the topsoil is from three to six feet deep. This is what the settlers found when they came. The only fertilizer our ancestors had was animal manure, and that was enough. Later, when commercial fertilizers came in, our grandfathers began to destroy the humus in their soil with overdoses of chemicals. Then they saw their error and began to turn under crops of green manure to build the topsoil back again.

At last town and city dwellers also are beginning to build back the topsoil that was farmed away or scraped away by bulldozers. It does not take too long if you establish several compost piles and simply save the leaves that fall on a city lot each year. Plain old mineral soil can be turned into topsoil, a little at a time. By mulching beds of flowers and shrubs and by adding some compost each year, we can restore our land to its former fertility.

There are all sorts of places where you can tuck away leaves back in distant corners and behind shrub borders, but not along the house foundation where they might encourage termites. When I went to see my cousin the other day, he had raked his extra leaves and pine needles into new flower-bed forms on his lawn and under the pines. The new "beds" of golden brown leaves and pine needles made an intriguing landscape in his back yard. As soon as the rains come and flatten the leaves underneath his shrubbery, he can rake up the "beds" which will decay faster than a deep compost pile, and scatter them underneath his shrubs, too.

Autumn rains will flatten the fattest beds of leaves down until you can hardly find them. Scatter a little soil over them now, and a little complete fertilizer if it is available, and you will feed your shrubbery and begin to build up soil faster than nature is doing it in the woods and forests.

ultimate size

As soon as the leaves are down, everybody starts raking away and making plans to plant trees and shrubs in the cool, sunshiny days from now till April. We are lucky in the South to be able to plant for nearly five months, except when it is raining or there is a deep snow.

My theme song in the fall is "Ultimate Size." As I told my class of fifty enthusiastic students, on a field trip across the old University of North Carolina campus not long ago, "You absolutely must know how big your trees and shrubs will grow before you can put them on a plan." At my lecture series in Winston-Salem, I filled one whole blackboard with my "sermon": "How Big Will It Grow?"

Little conifers and little broadleaved evergreens are so cute that we take them home from the nursery and stick them somewhere—very often without much planning. Many of the smallest are the very ones that will grow to be the biggest. Even Siberian wolfhounds are small when they are young!

We know that the southern magnolia (*Magnolia grandiflora*) and the sweet bay (*M. virginiana*) are two of our very biggest broadleaved evergreens. The hollies come next, and they will get to be big trees in ten years. Next down the scale are the big osmanthuses and the scrambling elaegnuses and Japanese privet (*Ligustrum lucidum*). Glossy privet (*L. japonicum*) grows more slowly and does not reach holly size. While camellias look small at first, and you think your rare ones will never grow, just visit an old camellia garden and see fifteen- to twenty-foot specimens!

Colorado spruces (*Picea pungens*) are so slow-growing that most of us do not worry about their ultimate size, but the Norway spruce (*P. abies*), all the pine trees, and hemlocks will make large trees in a hurry. Even our wild red cedars (*Juniperus virginiana*) will become big trees in a short time.

The beautiful false-cypresses (*Chamaecyparis*) or Retinisporas of catalogues are useful because they grow in ten to twenty years into medium-sized trees, usually less than twenty-five feet tall. They must not be incorporated in the foundation planting, however, as they were when they first came into nurseries forty years ago.

Many so-called dwarf forms of the evergreens and many of the very slow-growing trees and shrubs will ultimately grow to large sizes. The dwarf Pfitzer juniper is really just a slow grower and will eventually attain quite some size. It is no miniature. Even the dwarf Hinoki false-cypress (*C. nana*) will attain fifteen feet in thirty years. Only the conifers called *pigmaea* and *minima* are true diminutives. All this is not to cast aspersions upon so-called dwarf forms of trees and shrubs. These slightly smaller types are very desirable, but we must understand that they are not pygmies—merely slow growers.

witch-hazel time

When the settlers first came to this country, they were astounded at all the wonderful new plants they had never seen before. One of the bushes in the woods, for instance, was obviously "bewitched." For no reason at all, it would suddenly pop seeds out in all directions and scare the daylights out of anybody wandering in the forest. So they called it witch hazel. They were even more surprised when this same bush suddenly came into bloom about Thanksgiving time, after the leaves had fallen. Little bunches of yellow, stringy flowers scented the air for a long distance around. The scent reminded them of the odor of musk, so much sought after in those days in Europe.

The witch hazels are a joy to us today. The foliage turns beautiful colors in the autumn. The odor is a mixture of musk and lemon, powerful enough to scent up the woods and too strong for most people to bring into the house. Over in Missouri and Arkansas, there is a spring-flowering variety that blooms before anything else and serves as the harbinger of spring. This species is *Hamamelis vernalis* in the catalogues, while our eastern species is *H. virginiana*. There is a form of *virginiana* which is a large shrub or small tree, found mostly in the Lower South.

Though the flower odor of witch hazels is too strong for the house, the scent of the once-popular rubbing medicine made from it is delightful. Bay rum and witch hazel were the joys of the barber shop, where the final touch was that flourish of the bottle and light massage to the face with one of these pleasant scents.

The oriental witch hazels have somewhat larger flowers than their American kin. In China and Japan, they have long been prized for their late-winter to early spring blossoms. Some of them get to be twenty feet tall. They have been exhibited and have taken many prizes at the Royal Horticultural Society in London.

Try to plant your witch hazel in front of a dark background like a red cedar. The flowers are ephemeral and hard to see without something dark behind them.

december

tulips

Whether it be six or six hundred, tulips provide the most excitement in the spring garden. No other bulb runs to all the colors from violet through the reds and pinks to white and adds the yellows, too. The early kinds begin to flower right after crocuses, and the season runs through the spring till iris time.

You can touch up your spring garden with tulips from bulbs that are still in the stores. You may not find just what you want this late in the season, but any you plant will add color and zest. Be sure to soak the bulbs overnight or even for twenty-four hours to replace the moisture they lost when they were dried out for shipment from Holland and while they have lain in the bins in the store.

They bloom during the cool days of spring, overlapping with the daffodils, while the weather is still pleasant for garden visiting. When they are all in bloom, it is easy to see why the Dutch and Belgians went mad over them during the famous "tulip craze" between 1635 and 1637. One bulb of 'Semper Augustus' is said to have sold for 4,600 Dutch florins plus a new *caros* ("coach") with two "apple-greys"—the coach and horses to be delivered within a month, the money to be paid at once, even though the bulb was not to be delivered until later!

Tulips have a short growing season. During the few weeks when they have leaves on them, they must gather the food that is to make leaves and a flower bud for next year. One can see, then, that they must be planted in good, rich earth. If they are carelessly stuck into poor soil, they will flower and then vanish in a year or so. Planted six inches deep with four to six inches of rich soil beneath them, they will stay with you until this rich soil is depleted. The several small flowers they produce after the first year along with the main flower just add more color to a bed. Some of the wild tulips that send up multiple blossoms even the first year are becoming more and more popular.

Small gardens can be livened up by planting groups of six to ten bulbs here and there. In small groups like this, the drying foliage is not as noticeable as it is in a big bed planted exclusively to tulips.

Blue phlox, larkspur, pansies, Chinese forget-me-nots, nigella, and many other spring annuals can be either set out or seeded over the bulbs. Even if late-planted annuals do not bloom along with the tulips, they will provide a green ground cover and then grow up and hide the receding tulip foliage as it withers. Bulb catalogues provide us with pictures galore of tulip beds with accompanying plants. Do plant a few of the stunning water-lily tulips and the *greigii* hybrids.

wild tulips

The idea of wild tulips seems very farfetched, but the ancestors of our gorgeous modern tulips came from Turkey, Iran, Iraq, Russia, Afghanistan, and all across that part of the world. Just in the last few years some of the wild tulips have been available to us through the bulb companies and seed stores. These species tulips seem to like southern gardens. They like the hot summers and high ground temperatures—and drought.

Many gardeners have grown the delicate little deep-pink and white *Tulipa clusiana* called the lady tulip, and it seems to have settled down to stay for most people. It is surprising that this little flower has not been in general cultivation before now since the botanist Clusius flowered it in 1607! It is so delicate and graceful that the florists have been using it in France for years. Mountainous regions of Persia, Iran, Iraq, Afghanistan, and all the way to the terrible mountains of the Hindu Kush are its home. It increases by stolons, making a bigger and bigger patch.

A strange tulip indeed is *T. acuminata*. (The species tulips have not yet picked up common names the way *clusiana* did.) The long, stringy petals look as if someone had taken the scissors to the flowers, which are red and yellow. It is a real prize for flower arrangers.

There are numerous wild red tulips all through the Middle East. Most of them have a black blotch inside, with or without a yellow aura around it. In cool weather and on cloudy days only the red outsides show, but when it warms up or the sun comes out, these flowers open wide and show their black inside blotches. Such a combination demands your attention. Although it seems a bit artificial, some people plant white sweet alyssum over them as a ground cover. I have grown some of these red-and-black species and found them very tough and permanent as long as I have not allowed them to starve. Some of them are very early. They will bloom just as the snow melts over them in late winter. In catalogues they appear under names like *linifolia*, *princeps*, *praestans*, and *oculis-solis* ("sun's eye").

There are wild tulips in other colors. *Batalanii* is deep gold. *Urumiensis* is yellow and has many flowers to the stem. So do *turkestanica* and *dasystemon*. These newcomers can be grown to themselves in beds or groups until you get to know them. Then they can be placed in the garden wherever you fancy. Gardeners are getting very sophisticated these days and do not mind botanical names, but we shall surely find some common names for these botanical tulips. They are proving to be so permanent here in the South that our gardens will soon be as full of them as the fabulous gardens of the Persian princes.

photinas

Rated as one of the very handsomest of all the broadleaf evergreens is *Photinia serrulata*, a big shrub or small tree in our southern landscapes. The few red leaves that are always present among the green ones and the red new foliage make it the favorite of many gardeners.

Like many trees and shrubs in the rose family, photinias do not often flower and make seeds until they have some age, most of them not until they are about ten years old. When they are continually cut back and not allowed to grow to their normal size, they keep trying to attain maturity and are not able to bloom. Thousands of photinias can be seen growing in foundation plantings all over the South. They are not at all suited to such small spaces, and it is a big job to move them.

The other day, I saw something so brilliant in the winter sunshine that I was compelled to walk across a whole parking lot to see what it was. A mature photinia about twenty-five feet high was loaded down with huge corymbs of brilliant berries. Two trunks half the size of telephone poles gave the age of this magnificent specimen to be something like forty years. This superb photinia must have been planted way back in the twenties or early thirties when *P. serrulata* was introduced to this part of the South from my uncle J. van Lindley's nursery. On some of the campuses that I visit over the southern states from time to time, and also in cemeteries, these splendid photinias have grown to twenty or thirty feet and put on a magnificent winter show. We shall soon be using them in our Christmas decorations because the corymbs of tiny, red, apple-like fruits are as flat as the heads of elderberries and are very easy to manage in arrangements.

P. glabra, the smaller photinia we use in hedges, is also a beautiful shrub. It usually flowers at a smaller height. Its fruit is red too, but the smaller, duller foliage is not quite up to that of *serrulata*. Grown for its brilliant red new foliage that appears each time it is trimmed, this species is often called red top in Louisiana and Texas.

Some years ago, the old Fraser nursery in Alabama introduced a beautiful photinia (×*fraseri*) which seems to be a cross between these two species. The new foliage is red and about the size of that of *serrulata*. The hydrid has been popular and can be bought in most nurseries or on plant stands. In Australia, Hazlewood's Nursery has produced the same cross and called it 'Robusta'. My friends the Hilliers offer two forms of Fraser's cross called 'Birmingham' and 'Red Robin' as well as the Australian 'Robusta'. They note that the latter stands the cold best in England.

If you should by chance run into a big bush with the typical flat heads of photinia berries and no winter foliage, you may have discovered one of the nonevergreen species. There are a few in the South.

lilies

Fat lily bulbs are in the stores along with the tulips and hyacinths. True lilies look like big handfuls of scales hung together at the bottom by a few roots. They demonstrate well the fact that a bulb is really made up of sections compacted together on a short stem and a bit of root.

If you will think of lilies as big perennials and prepare the soil for them accordingly, you will succeed in keeping them from year to year. Drainage, leaf mold, and some charcoal are what lilies like most of all. They are ravenous for food all the time—even when they seem to be sleeping under the ground. Jan de Graaff, our Oregon specialist, says that nothing is as good as the traditional well-rotted cow manure for lilies. He prefers bone meal and cottonseed meal next and 5-10-5 commercial fertilizer if you cannot get manure or cottonseed meal. He also recommends a tablespoonful of wood ashes per bulb every year. Any of these can be mixed with the soil when the bulbs are planted and then scattered over the bed each following year.

Since lilies look best in groups, they may be planted in small areas prepared especially for them. Dig out the soil and either replace it with good loam plus fertilizer, or make up some soil of one-half garden soil, one-fourth leaf mold or peat moss, and one-fourth coarse (not fine) sand. There should be at least six inches of good soil underneath your bulbs and about four inches above them. (Madonna lilies are usually planted "more shallow.") The bed should be mulched with leaves, and the mulch can be left on and renewed yearly.

If we regard lily bulbs as large perennial roots, we will not make the mistake of letting them dry out like tulips or daffodils or gladiolas. They should be kept in very slightly moist peat moss or sawdust until you are ready to plant them. Many gardeners who know lily culture well simply pot their bulbs right away, if they cannot plant them out, and bury the pots in the ground until the beds are ready for them.

Lilies are usually found growing amongst or in front of shrubs or other plants in the wild. The tall stems look most natural coming up through something. Out by themselves, they look bare. Although most of the lilies at Savill Gardens near Windsor Castle were out of bloom when I saw them last, even the tall bunches of stems were beautiful back in the beds of flowers and in front of various kinds of shrubs. At this garden, which is famous for its lilies, they have combined them with big clumps of hostas here and there.

tender plants

Southern gardeners are accustomed to hearing that "we are going to have a cold winter." What is a "cold winter"? We never have the sustained low temperatures over long periods which are common in the North. Our cold periods come and go, with mild intervals. But it is the short periods of low temperatures that get us excited because they kill back our tender plants.

No southerner can resist growing figs and Cape jessamines. Who would be without ginger lilies? It is a challenge to grow tender plants, and the discussion as to which side of the house is best for them is always a lively one.

Back in the beginning of this century and, records show, in the last one, there were some prolonged periods of low temperatures that killed the figs to the ground. Up in the hill and mountain country, people made a sort of wigwam of cornstalks around their fig trees. They placed the stalks in amongst the branches and then added an outer layer a foot or so thick. When I was a child, I thought these cornstalk tents were beautiful in the orchard and garden.

When cold periods below freezing last more than a day or so, the ground begins to freeze, and tender bulbs are apt to be killed. The Peruvian daffodil is the most subject to cold of all our tender bulbs. While the bulb itself may not be killed, the flower buds are destroyed by low temperatures. It is really best to dig and store them inside to be sure of bloom. Only very prolonged cold periods will damage montbretia or gladiolas. To be sure of their safety, just put a six- to twelve-inch leaf mulch over them till spring.

Protecting Cape jasmines and other forms of gardenias can be done by erecting a little chicken-wire fence around the bushes with a plastic cover over it to fend off the winds. If you put on a top, be sure to leave an opening for heat to escape when the sun shines.

Ginger lilies and other tender plants will come through our winters with a deep leaf mulch. It is the evergreen spider lilies, sternbergias, and amaryllises that have the worst time in cold winters. All of these bulbs must have winter sunshine to develop their flower buds. In the North, where sternbergias can be grown if protected, gardeners put salt hay over them in winter. Here in the South our spider lilies are often damaged by the few cold spells that last more than two or three days. Pine tops laid over them seem to pull them through and preserve enough flower buds for us to have blossoms in summer and fall.

variegated ivies

The ivies of all kinds with partly yellow or partly white leaves are very attractive in contrast to all the broadleaf evergreens we have. They lighten up the greens like flowers in winter the same way that aucubas do. Once in a while, one can find the golden-edged form of the sweet ivy in pots on plant stands. This one may have a label that says *Hedera colchica dentato-variegata*. Buy it; it is a real treasure because it is not gaudy but gives just that touch of yellow amongst the greens that is not too much.

Canary Island ivy (*H. canariensis*) has a thinner leaf than either English (*H. helix*) or sweet ivy (*H. colchica*) and comes in a number of blotch-leaved varieties—some partly white and some partly yellow. Canary Island ivy is hardy here in the South. Some old gardens and cemeteries have masses of it. The large leaves are longish, as a rule, and without the big lobes of all the other kinds.

Some of the most beautiful of the variegated varieties are 'Goldheart', with a golden patch in the middle of the leaf approximating the shape of the leaf; 'Gold Dust', with a wrinkled leaf that has a dusted effect all over; 'Glacier', with white-edged leaves and white running back into the center—a beautiful design; 'Heise-Denmark', with the same cream arrangement as 'Glacier' but with leaves that are beautiful little things—almost heart-shaped; 'Marginata', with creamy edges and a sort of grey-green effect over the rest of the leaves. 'Marginata' is a very, very old variety of ivy, a favorite even before Mr. Shirley Hibberd wrote his beautiful book *The Ivy, a Monograph* in 1893. Ivy specialists think this old variety is one of the very toughest. There seem to be many variations on it these days.

Besides the above list of variegateds, as ivy fans call them, you will find the popular 'Sub-Marginata', 'Little Diamond', 'California Gold', and the mottled 'Marmorata Elegans'. All of the variegateds here mentioned are relatively small-leaved.

You can find an abundance of types in plant stores now since house plants have become so poplar. There are the "heart-shaped" varieties, the "fan," the "bird's-foot," and the "curlies." If you are a real ivy enthusiast, you might like to join the American Ivy Society, National Center for American Horticulture, Mount Vernon, Virginia 22121.

tree space

Tree lovers hate to see fine shade trees suffering from lack of room. When trees that will attain any size, such as oaks and maples, are planted too close to buildings, they have only a limited lifetime, because after they begin to reach maturity, their limbs must be cut back and their natural form distorted. Before they are really grown, they are doomed. Thirty-five feet from a building is not too far to plant a future big shade tree. This far from a structure, the tree can be pruned to fit the space it will occupy. If shortening the limbs on the building side distorts the specimen, tree surgeons can balance it by lightening the limbs on the opposite side.

Ride around town—or better still walk around—and take a look at the shade trees in yards and gardens. The best specimens are those which have enough room to develop their limb and branch systems fully. Usually, these trees are standing some twenty or more feet from houses and from telephone wires. The tulip tree (*Liriodendron tulipifera*), often called tulip poplar, and the hickories are exceptions because these trees grow rather straight up and do not need so much space to spread. Hickories do not grow off very fast, but tulips do—as fast as any native tree. There are numerous native medium-sized and small trees which can be grown in limited spaces. We in the South have neglected some of these beautiful and interesting natives. Nurseries do not offer them to us because we do not ask for them.

New housing developments have been planting black or river birches (*Betula nigra*) everywhere because landscapers have discovered that they can easily go to creek banks and remove nice young birches, bare-root, out of the sand and transplant them successfully. The bark on the young trees is a handsome pinkish beige, and the trees are very tolerant of the bad situations where they usually get planted. In maturity, these trees have darker bark which accounts for the name black birch. In the North, white birch (*B. papyrifera*) is the choice, but our river birch is also beautiful.

For very restricted spaces, the little ironwood or hornbeam (*Carpinus caroliniana*) and the small hop hornbeam (*Ostrya virginiana*) are graceful shade trees. The chinquapin (*Castanea pumila*) is another small tree that has beautiful foliage as well as interesting, edible nuts. The foliage of this one looks like that of our lost chestnut tree. The box elder (*Acer negundo*)—really a smallish maple—is a quick-growing species that can ultimately attain quite some size but remains small for a long time.

For quite small areas, dogwood, redbud, and the snowdrop or silverbell (*Halesia carolina*) will provide both shade and showy flowers. Sourwood (*Oxydendrum arboreum*) is more upright than spreading. Even blackjack (*Quercus marilandica*) and turkey oaks (*Q. laevis*) are beautiful when they are grown as specimens, as they often are in areas where they are plentiful. All of these native trees will outlast the oriental flowering cherries, peaches, and plums.

land of evergreens

Southern yards and gardens and our southern woods are a feast of evergreens in winter. In addition to our own native pines, magnolias,

hollies, and numerous other trees and shrubs, we have many evergreens from all over the world.

When Thomas Hariot, Sir Walter Raleigh's "surveyor," saw the many
new kinds of evergreens in the coastal country of North Carolina and
Virginia, he could think of nothing to call them except some names he
already knew, so he called each of them some kind of bay or laurel. In
his description, written for the English readers, he described a number
of evergreens and then just gave up—there seemed to be so many new
kinds—and said simply, "The rest is bays."

The English, in the sixteenth century, were looking for new kinds of
wood for their wooden houses and ships. They were dazzled with all the
new trees and shrubs in the New World. When the settlers made their
way into the mountains in the seventeenth and eighteenth centuries,
they called everything evergreen some kind of laurel or some kind of
ivy. In the Blue Ridges they seem to have named their new shrubs
"laurel." West of the Blue Ridges, everything evergreen was "ivy."

Today, we have combined our finest evergreens with those from
many other parts of the world to adorn our landscapes. Tall cunninghamias
and ferny cryptomerias from China grow perfectly in the mild southern
winter. At home in China, cunninghamias are used for coffins because
they are resistant to worms and decay. The wood of both of these
elegant conifers is made into valuable lumber that needs no decay-
proofing chemicals.

The common spruce of Norway, (*Picea abies*) has always been popular in the South. It grows quickly into the traditional Christmas-tree
form and was once used, both North and South, as a commercial tree
for the holiday season. Down here in the South, it is beautiful for about
fifty years and then plays out in our heat. Although it is rare, we have a
few very fine specimens of the oriental spruce (*P. orientalis*). This one
comes from eastern Europe around the Black Sea and likes the heat
here.

Most popular of all, of course, are the exotic true cedars. Because of
its connection with Solomon and the Temple, the cedar of Lebanon,
(*Cedrus libani*) has always been a favorite tree. When the deodar cedar,
(*C. deodara*) was discovered, it was immediately sought after because
of its soft, graceful, silvery appearance. Not many people know the
extremely handsome Atlas cedar (*C. atlantica*). Any eye-catching silvery cedar that you run across is likely to be "blue" Atlas cedar. This is
one of the "diamonds" of all coniferous trees.

pleasures of christmas decorating

One of the greatest pleasures of Christmas time is decorating the house and the church. Nothing lifts the spirits more than to walk into a building and find that greens and berries have been brought inside.

In planning your decorations, it is well to remember that it is the contrast between the dark greens and the light and silvery and gray greens that is most effective. This is especially true where your decorations will be in relatively dark places with no light on them. In churches and auditoriums where they are to be seen at some distance, just plain masses of dark green may look monotonous without the addition of gray or silver foliage or artificial ornaments for contrast. Collect a variety of shades and take them into the house and see how they will look before you combine them. If you are disappointed with the way they show up, you can often solve the problem by increasing the electric lights in the house.

There are so many beautiful dried weeds in fields and gardens that we can find something new to use every year. Goldenrods, silverrods, milkweed, and grasses are extremely effective in lightening up heavy masses of greenery.

Perhaps the commonest gray or silvery conifers are deodar cedar trees (*Cedrus deodara*). When you steal some of this material from your trees, do not snip off the tips of the big branches; take instead some bits from the longest branchlets. If the tips of low branches are shortened, you may deform the tree's shape for the future.

Pfitzer junipers can easily be robbed of some good sprays. Where the branches are thickest—sometimes a bit too thick for all of them to develop—you can reach down inside the bush and cut out a whole branch as much as two feet long. When you remove even the shorter ones, cut them off down inside the bush instead of just bobbing off the end, because this practice soon thickens up Pfitzers too much.

The common English laurel (*Prunus laurocerasus*) that used to be so prevalent in southern plantings has about disappeared because it grew too big too fast. Like Japanese privet, however, this beautiful broadleaf does not mind—in fact, needs—yearly touching up. English laurel is one of the most elegant of all broadleaf evergreens for decorations. Maybe you can find one in a planting somewhere. The foliage is large but not as coarse as that of the southern magnolia.

Bring in your greens and throw them in the tub overnight. Put a weight on them and cover them completely with water. The next day skin the stems up on two sides for a few inches and throw them back into the water for awhile before you take them out to use them.

spruces and firs

Of all the Christmas trees one can buy, Fraser's fir (*Abies fraseri*) is the most elegant. Called balsam and she-balsam in the high southern mountains where it grows, it provides most of the fragrant needles for the balsam pillows we buy in the mountains in summer. The early settlers who penetrated into the high mountains of Virginia, North Carolina, and Tennessee noticed the large blisters of clear, sweet resin in the wood of these trees. Since the wood of the spruces did not have this resin, they called Fraser's fir she-balsam and red spruce (*Picea rubra*) he-balsam.

Red spruce and Fraser's fir grow mostly at elevations above 5,000 feet. To see them, you will have to go up to "the Grandfather," "the Roan," "the Blacks," "Clingman's Dome" and "the Smokies." There are only a few other places in the South where they grow. Forests of spruce and fir are called balsam groves up there. In summer, when you walk through one of these heavenly areas over the needles underneath the trees, the odor of balsam surrounds you everywhere, and you will never want to leave! No wonder they call it God's country.

The she-balsam is in deep trouble in our mountains. The spruce-gall aphid is destroying it apace, and the only protection for it is to spray the trees every year and poison the aphids before they can get under way. Large areas are being protected with spray by the Forest Service while they try to determine how to save this species from destruction. The bluish silvery bloom of the tree is one of the most elegant things one sees in the high mountains. Young trees are particularly showy, especially when the undersides of the needles are seen. Spruces have a stubbier look and none of this elegant bloom and are yellow green.

Since Fraser's fir is in trouble in the forests, we are most fortunate that the Christmas-tree farmers long ago chose this species to grow and cut for our houses for the holiday season. They grow them by the thousands in the mountains and send them all over the United States. You will find them on the stands now as cut Christmas trees. Even if they are balled and burlapped, Fraser's firs will not grow for you unless you live above 3,000 feet. They long for the cool mountains, home of the Cherokees.

When your Christmas tree begins to dry up, and you are ready to remove it from the house, by all means do not throw it away! Put it in the garage where it can dry out completely. As it turns yellow and dries, you will begin to smell the delightful balsam in the needles. Shake them onto a cloth or paper, let them dry some more, and then make your very own balsam pillows or sachets out of some coarse material which will allow the odor to escape.

chinese hollies

One of the most beautiful and useful ornamental plants sent home to England from China by Robert Fortune in 1846 was the Chinese holly (*Ilex cornuta*). Fortune had found it growing all along the Yangtse River as far up as Hupeh, a large river basin, whence have come many superb plants to our gardens.

It is a little surprising that we in the United States did not receive Chinese holly until after the First World War when the Department of Agriculture began to send seeds around. That wonderful plantsman, Mr. E. A. McIlhenny, at Avery Island, Louisiana, was quick to raise the new plant from seeds. He soon found several variations among his seedlings—two of them yellow berried and one of which he named 'Jungle Gardens' for his place. Another variety he called 'Rotunda', and he sent seeds of it to the U.S.D.A. Division of Plant Exploration and Introduction.

'Rotunda' is a popular evergreen in nurseries because of its perfectly rounded, dense form. The large, shiny green mounds are spectacular in many southern landscapes today. Like Pfitzer junipers, however, these beautiful bushes are appearing in spaces that are far too small. They cannot be kept down to small sizes forever.

The normal Chinese holly with its five spines and glossy leaves would be a glorious thing, even if no special forms had ever been found of it. We all know, now, that these trees will grow to very large sizes even when held back by pruning. Perhaps the greatest virtue of all the forms of this superb holly lies in the thick wax covering on the leaves that makes the whole shrub or tree exceedingly sun, heat, and drought resistant. They can even withstand the terrific heat and full sun in front of concrete buildings in midsummer where most other hollies would scorch.

Burford holly is simply a one-spined variety of the Chinese. This variety is one of the most popular of all hollies these days. Burford was sent to Mr. T. W. Burford, a cemetery keeper in Atlanta, years ago. Pleased with its small leaves and only one sticker, he recognized it as a fine plant, and it was named after him. The late Mr. S. R. Howell of Knoxville, Tennessee, first propagated Burford, and Dr. Jesse de France (whom I assisted with his doctoral thesis on broadleaf evergreens) published a description in the *National Horticultural Magazine*. This is what it takes to launch a fine, new variety. Don't let the small leaves of Burford deceive you into thinking it is a dwarf; it grows to the same twenty or more feet of the standard *cornuta*!

There are, today, many fine new varieties of Chinese holly. The seeds yield many variations. Plant some and see what you get!

bibliography

Allan, Mea. *E. A. Bowles and His Garden.* London: Faber & Faber, 1973.

Bloom, Alan. *Hardy Perennials for the Garden.* London: Faber & Faber, 1957.

Bowles, E. A. *My Garden in Autumn and Winter.* London: T. C. & E. C. Jack, 1914.

    My Garden in Spring. London, 1914. Reprint. London: Theophrastus, 1971.

    My Garden in Summer. London: T. C. & E. C. Jack, 1914.

Brown, Clair Alan. *Louisiana Trees and Shrubs.* Baton Rouge: Claitor's Book Store, 1955.

Burbidge, F. W., and Booker, J. G. *The Narcissus, Its History and Culture.* London: L. Reeve & Co., 1875.

Classified List and International Register of Daffodil Names. London: Royal Horticultural Society, 1969.

Coker, William Chamber, and Totten, Henry Roland. *Trees of the Southeastern States.* Chapel Hill: University of North Carolina Press, 1934.

Dormon, Caroline. *Flowers Native to the Deep South.* Baton Rouge: Claitor's Book Store, 1958.

    Natives Preferred. Baton Rouge: Claitor's Book Store, 1965.

Elliott, Stephen. *Sketch of the Botany of South Carolina and Georgia.* Charleston, S. C., 1821–24.

Evelyn, John. *Acetaria, a discourse of sallets.* London, 1699.

Gerard, John. *The Herbal or General history of plantes.* London, 1596.

Gray, Alec. *Miniature Daffodils.* Forest Hills, N. Y.: Transatlantic Arts, Inc., 1955.

Hibbard, Shirley. *The Ivy, a Monograph.* 2d ed. London: W. H. & L. Collingridge, 1893.

Historical Sketch Book and Guide to New Orleans, edited and compiled by several of the leading writers of the New Orleans Press. New York: Will H. Coleman, 1885.

Hume, H. Harold. *Camellias, Kinds and Culture.* New York: Macmillan, 1951.

Hurst, C. C. "History of Garden Roses." *Journal of the Royal Horticultural Society,* March, July, August, 1941.

Huxley, Anthony. *Garden Perennials and Water Plants.* New York: Macmillan, 1971.

Jefferson, Thomas. *Garden Book, 1766–1824, with relevant extracts from his other writings,* annotated by Edwin Morris Betts. Philadelphia: The American Philosophical Society, 1944.

Jordan, Alexis, and Fourreau, Jules. *Icones ad floram Europae.* 3 vols. Paris, 1866–[70].

Lawrence, Elizabeth. *Gardens in Winter.* New York: Harper, 1961.

    The Little Bulbs: A Tale of Two Gardens. New York: Criterion Books, 1957.

    A Southern Garden. 2d ed., rev. Chapel Hill: University of North Carolina Press, 1967.

Lelièvre, J. F. *Nouveau Jardinier de la Louisiane.* New Orleans: J. F. Lelièvre, 1838.

Mitchell, Allan. *A Field Guide to the Trees of Northern Britain and Europe.* London: Wm. Collins Sons and Co., Ltd., 1974.

Monardes, Nicolas. *Joyful Newes out of the Newe found World.* Translated by John Frampton. London: W. Norton, 1577.

Parkinson, John. *Paradisi in Sole, Paradisus Terrestris.* London, 1629.

Redouté, Pierre-Joseph. *Les Roses: décrites par C. A. Thory.* Paris [?], 1817–24.

Thomas, Graham. *The Old Shrub Roses.* London: Phoenix House, Ltd., 1961.

    Perennial Garden Plants. London: J. M. Dent and Sons, Ltd., 1976.

    Shrub Roses of Today. London: Phoenix House, Ltd., 1962.

Underwood, Mrs. Desmond. *Grey and Silver Plants.* London: Collins, 1971.

Wilson, Ernest Henry. *Aristocrats of the Garden.* Boston: The Stratford Company, 1926.

    China, Mother of Gardens. Boston: The Stratford Co., 1929.

    If I Were to Make a Garden. Boston: The Stratford Co., 1931.

    More Aristocrats of the Garden. Boston: The Stratford Co., 1931.

Wilson, Helen VanPelt, and Bell, Leonie. *The Fragrant Year.* New York: Crown Publishers, Inc., Bonanza Books, 1967.

Wyman, Donald. *Trees for American Gardens.* Revised and enlarged ed. New York: Macmillan, 1965.

index

about the author

William Lanier Hunt has written and spoken widely on gardening and is
a respected consultant to botanical gardens throughout the South. He is
the donor of the W. L. Hunt Arboretum at the North Carolina Botanical
Garden, honorary president of the Southern Garden History Society,
a member of the Royal Horticultural Society of England, and a life
member of the International Dendrology Society.